WHY MEN
DON'T LISTEN

WOMEN CAN'T
READ MAPS

Allan & Barbara Pease

Copyright © Allan Pease 2001

The right of Allan Pease to be identified as the author
of this work has been asserted by him in accordance with
the Copyright, Designs and Patents Act 1988.

First published in Great Britain in 1999
by Orion-PTI

This edition published in 2001
by Orion Books Ltd,
Orion House, 5 Upper St Martin's Lane,
London WC2H 9EA

An Hachette Livre UK company

Reissued 2006

20 19 18 17 16

A CIP catalogue record for this book is available
from the British Library.

ISBN 978-0-7528-4619-4

Designed by Staziker Jones, Cardiff

Printed by Clays Ltd, St Ives plc

The Orion Publishing Group's policy is to use papers that
are natural, renewable and recyclable products and
made from wood grown in sustainable forests. The logging
and manufacturing processes are expected to conform to
the environmental regulations of the country of origin.

www.orionbooks.co.uk

Why not use Allan Pease as guest speaker for your next conference or seminar?

Pease International (Australia) Pty Ltd
Pease International (UK) Ltd

P.O. Box 1260
Buderim 4556
Queensland
AUSTRALIA
Tel: ++61 7 5445 5600
Fax: ++61 7 5445 5688

Liberty House
16 Newbold Terrace
Leamington Spa CV 32 4 EG
UNITED KINGDOM
Tel: ++44 (0) 1926 889900
Fax: ++44 (0) 1926 421100

email: (Aust) info@peaseinternational.com
           (UK) ukoffice@peaseinternational.com
website: www.peaseinternational.com

Also by Allan Pease:

Video Programs
Body Language Series
Silent Signals
The Interview
How to Make Appointments by Telephone

DVD Programs
The Best of Body Language
How to Develop Powerful Communication—Managing the
Differences Between Men and Women

Audio Programs
The Four Personality Styles
How to Make Appointments by Telephone
How to Remember Names, Faces & Lists
Why Men Don't Listen and Women Can't Read Maps
Questions are the Answers

Books
The Definitive Book of Body Language
Why Men Don't Listen & Women Can't Read Maps
Why Men Lie and Women Cry
Why Men Can Only Do One Thing At A Time & Women Never Stop
Talking
How Compatible Are You?
Talk Language
Write Language
Questions are the Answers
The Bumper Book of Rude & Politically Incorrect Jokes
Politically Incorrect Jokes Men Love

By Allan & Barbara Pease

The Definitive Book of Body Language
Why Men Don't Have a Clue and Women Always Need
    More Shoes
Why Men Don't Listen and Women Can't Read Maps
Questions are the Answers
Talk Language
Why Men Can Only Do one Thing at a Time and
    Women Never Stop Talking

CONTENTS

ACKNOWLEDGMENTS

We wish to thank the following people who have contributed directly, indirectly, and often unknowingly to this book.

Ray & Ruth Pease, Bill & Beat Suter, Alison & Mike Tilley, Jaci Eliott, Stella Brocklesby, Paula & Natasha Thompson, Col & Jill Haste, Dr Desmond Morris, Prof Detlef Linke, Carole Tonkinson, Prof Alan Garner, Bronia Szczygiel, John & Sue Macintosh, Kevin Austin, Dr John Tickell, Dr Rosie King, Dr Barry Kitchen, Diana Ritchie, Cadbury Schweppes, Amanda Gore, Esther Rantzen, Melissa, Cameron & Jasmine Pease, Adam Sellars, Gary Skinner, Mike & Carol Pease, Andy Clarke, Len & Sue Smith, Dr Dennis Waitley, Fiona & Michael Hedger, Christine Maher, Ray Martin, Dr Rudi Brasch, Prof Stephen Dain, Christine Craigie, Dr Themi Garagounas, Prof Dennis Burnham, Prof Barbara Gillham, Bryan Cockerill, Leanne Wilson, Geoff Arnold, Lisa Tierney, Robyn McCormick, Kerri-Anne Kennerley, Geoff Burch, Jonathan Norman, Marie Ricot, Julie Fenton, Nick Symons, Richard & Linda Denny, Angela & Sheila Watson-Challis, Simon Howard, Tom Kenyon-Slaney, Tony and Patrica Earle, Darley Anderson, Sue Irvine, Leanne Christie, Anita & Dave Kite, Barry Toepher, Bert Newton, Brendan Walsh, Carrie Siipola, Debbie Tawse, Celia Barnes, Christina Peters, Hannelore Federspiel, David & Jan Goodwin, Eunice and Ken Worden, Frank and Cavill Boggs, Graham and Tracey

Dufty, Graham Shiels, Grant Sexton, Kaz Lyons, Barry Markoff, Peter Rosetti, Max Hitchins, Debbie Mehrtens, Jack & Valerie Collis, John Allanson, John Hepworth, Pru Watts, Michael & Sue Rabbit, Michael & Sue Burnett, Michael & Kaye Goldring, Mike Schoettler, Peter & Jill Gosper, Rachel Jones, Ros & Simon Townsend, Sussan Hawryluk, Sue Williams, Terry & Tammy Butler, W. Mitchell, Walter Dickman, Bea Pullar, Alan Collinson, Russell Jeffery, Sandra & Loren Watts, Katrina Flynn, Luke Causby, Peter Draper, Scott Gilmour, Janet Gilmour, Lisa Petrich, Geoff Weatherburn, Dawn Eccles-Simkins, David Orchard, Donn Guthrie, Chris Stewart, Howard Gibbs, Sue McIlwraith, Jules Di Maio, Nathan Haynes, Michael Kelly, Gary Larson, Dorie Simmonds and Trevor Dolby.

INTRODUCTION

A Sunday Drive

It was a sunny Sunday afternoon as Bob and Sue set out with their three teenage daughters on a lazy drive down to the beach. Bob was at the wheel and Sue sat beside him, turning towards the back every few minutes to join in the animated series of conversations going on among their daughters. To Bob, it sounded as if they were all talking at once, creating an incessant barrage of noise that just didn't make any sense at all. Eventually, he'd had enough.

'Can you lot please shut up!' he yelled.

There was a stunned silence.

'Why?' asked Sue, eventually.

'Because I'm trying to drive!' he replied, exasperated.

The women looked at each other in complete confusion.

'Trying to drive?' they mumbled.

They could not see any connection between their conversation and his ability to drive. He couldn't understand why they were all speaking simultaneously, sometimes on different subjects, with none of them appearing to listen.

Why couldn't they just keep quiet and let him concentrate on driving? Their talking had already caused him to miss the last turn-off on the highway.

The fundamental problem here is simple: men and women are different. Not better or worse – just different. Scientists, anthropologists and sociobiologists have known this for years, but they have also been painfully aware that to express this knowledge publicly in such a politically correct world could turn them into social pariahs. Society today is determined to believe that men and women possess exactly the same skills, aptitudes and potentials – just as science, ironically, is beginning to prove they are completely different.

And where does this leave us? As a society, on extremely shaky ground. It's only by understanding the differences between men and women that we can really start building on our collective strengths – rather than on our individual weaknesses. In this book, we seize upon the enormous advances that have recently been made in human evolutionary science and show how the lessons learned apply to male and female relationships. The conclusions we unearth are controversial. They are confronting. They are, occasionally, extremely disturbing. But they give us all a solid and thorough understanding of the many strange things that happen between men and women. If only Bob and Sue had read it before they had set out ...

Why Writing This Book Was So Tough

This book took us three years, and more than 400,000 kilometres, to write. In the course of our research, we studied papers, interviewed experts and gave seminars throughout Australia, New Zealand, Singapore, Thailand, Hong Kong, Malaysia, England, Scotland, Ireland, Italy, Greece, Germany, Holland, Spain, Turkey, the USA, South Africa, Botswana, Zimbabwe, Zambia, Namibia, Angola, Switzerland, Austria, Finland, Indonesia, Bulgaria, Saudi Arabia, Poland, Hungary, Borneo, Russia, Belgium, France, Japan and Canada.

One of the most difficult tasks was getting public and private organisations to give their opinions on the facts. For example, fewer than 1% of all commercial airline pilots are female. When we tried to discuss this with airline officials, many were too terrified to offer an opinion for fear of being accused of being sexist or anti-female. Many said 'no comment' and some organisations even made threats about their names being mentioned in our book. Women executives were generally more obliging, although many took an immediately defensive position and saw this research as an attack on feminism without even knowing what it was about. Some of the authoritative opinions we have documented were obtained 'off the record' from corporate executives and university professors in dimly-lit rooms, behind closed doors, with guarantees that they were not being quoted nor their organisations named. Many had two opinions – their politically correct public opinion and their real opinion, which was 'not to be quoted'.

You will find this book sometimes challenging, sometimes startling, but always fascinating. While it is based on hard scientific evidence, we have used everyday conversations, beliefs and scenarios that range from the humorous to the downright hilarious to make sure it's fun to read. We have tried to boil all the evidence down into the simplest explanations while, at the same time, avoiding oversimplification. This approach makes the information easily accessible for most people, but can annoy others in the science world who would prefer to read a science journal. Our objective in writing this book is to help you learn more about both yourself and the opposite sex, so that your interaction and relationships can be more fulfilling, enjoyable and satisfying.

One driving organisation measured gender differences in reverse parking ability and did comparisons in several countries. Their results were so astounding that when the report was released they were inundated with complaints that they were sexist and racist. The report was immediately withdrawn and locked away, never to be seen again, as it was clearly bad for business. We obtained a copy of this study and will discuss the results but, for legal and ethical reasons, we can't reveal the source.

This book is dedicated to all the men and women who

have ever sat up at 2am pulling their hair out as they plead with their partners, 'But *why* don't you understand?' Relationships fail because men still don't understand why a woman can't be more like a man, and women expect their men to behave just like they do. Not only will this book help you come to grips with the opposite sex, it'll help you understand yourself. And how you can both lead happier, healthier and more harmonious lives as a result.

Barbara and Allan Pease

CHAPTER 1
SAME SPECIES, DIFFERENT WORLDS

The Evolution of a Magnificent Creature

Men and women are different. Not better or worse – different. Just about the only thing they have in common is that they belong to the same species. They live in different worlds, with different values and according to quite different sets of rules. Everyone knows this, but very few people, particularly men, are willing to admit it. The truth, however, is most definitely out there. Look at the evidence. Around 50% of marriages end in divorce in Western countries and most serious relationships stop short of becoming long-term. Men and women of every culture, creed and hue constantly argue over their partners' opinions, behaviour, attitudes and beliefs.

Some Things Are Obvious

When a man goes to a toilet, he usually goes for one reason and one reason only. Women use toilets as social lounges and therapy rooms. Women who go to a toilet as strangers can come out best friends and lifelong buddies. But everyone would be instantly suspicious of the man who called out, 'Hey Frank, I'm going to the toilet. You wanna come with me?'

Men dominate TV remote controls and flick through the channels; women don't mind watching the commercials. Under pressure, men drink alcohol and invade other countries; women eat chocolate and go shopping.

Women criticise men for being insensitive, uncaring, not listening, not being warm and compassionate, not talking, not giving enough love, not being committed to relationships, wanting to have sex rather than make love, turning the temperature down, and leaving the toilet seat up.

Men criticise women about their driving, for not being able to read street directories, for turning maps upside down, for their lack of a sense of direction, for talking too much without getting to the point, for not initiating sex often enough, turning the temperature up, and for leaving the toilet seat down. Men can never find a pair of socks but their CDs are in alphabetical order. Women can always find the missing set of car keys, but rarely the most direct route to their destination. Men think they're the most sensible sex. Women *know* they are.

How many men does it take to change a roll of toilet paper? It's unknown. It's never happened.

Men marvel at the way a woman can walk into a room full of people and give an instant commentary on everyone; women can't believe men are so unobservant. Men are amazed how a woman can't see a red flashing oil light on the car dashboard but can spot a dirty sock in a dark corner 50 metres away. Women are bewildered by men who can consistently parallel park a car in a tight spot using a rear-view mirror, but can never find the G-spot.

If a woman is out driving and gets lost, she'll stop and ask for directions. To a man, this is a sign of weakness. He'll drive round in circles for hours, muttering things like, 'I've found a new way to get there' or 'I'm in the general area' and 'Hey, I recognise that petrol station!'

Different Job Specs

Men and women have evolved differently because they had to. Men hunted, women gathered. Men protected, women nurtured. As a result, their bodies and brains evolved in completely different ways.

As their bodies physically changed to adapt to their specific functions, so did their minds. Men grew taller and stronger than most women, while their brains developed to suit their tasks. Women were mostly content for men to work away as they kept the cave fires burning, and their brains evolved to cope with their function in life.

Over millions of years, the brain structures of men and women thus continued to change in different ways. Now, we know the sexes process information differently. They think differently. They believe different things. They have different perceptions, priorities and behaviours.

To pretend otherwise, is a recipe for heartache, confusion and disillusionment all your life.

The 'Stereotype' Argument

Since the late 1980s, there has been an explosion of research into male and female differences and the way both the male and female brains work. For the first time ever, advanced computer brainscanning equipment has allowed us to see the brain operating 'live' and, with that peek into the vast landscape of the human mind, provided us with many of the answers to the questions about male and female differences. The research discussed in this book has been collected from studies in scientific, medical, psychological and sociological studies and it all points clearly to one thing: All things are not equal; men and women are different. For most of the 20th Century those differences were explained away by social conditioning; that is, we are who we are because of our parents' and teachers' attitudes which, in turn, reflected the attitudes of their society. Baby girls were dressed in pink and given dolls to play with; baby boys were dressed in blue and given toy soldiers and football jerseys. Young girls were cuddled and touched while boys were thumped on the back and told not to cry. Until recently, it was believed that when a baby was born its mind was a clean slate on which its teachers could write its choices and preferences. The biological evidence now available, however, shows a somewhat different picture of why we think the way we do. It shows convincingly that it is our hormones and brain wiring that are largely responsible for our attitudes, preferences and behaviour. This means that if boys and girls grew up on a deserted island with no organised society or parents to guide them, girls would still cuddle, touch, make friends and play with dolls, while boys would compete mentally and physically with each other and form groups with a clear hierarchy.

The wiring of our brain in the womb

and the effect of hormones will

determine how we think and behave.

As you will see, the way our brains are wired and the hormones pulsing through our bodies are the two factors that largely dictate, long before we are born, how we will think and behave. Our instincts are simply our genes determining how our bodies will behave in given sets of circumstances.

Is it All a Male Conspiracy?

Since the 1960s a number of pressure groups have tried to persuade us to buck our biological legacy. They claim that governments, religions and education systems have added up to nothing more than a plot by men to suppress women, colluding to keep good women down. Keeping women pregnant was a way of controlling them even more.

Certainly, historically, that's how it appears. But the question needs to be asked: If women and men are identical, as these groups claim, how could men ever have achieved such total dominance over the world? The study of how the brain works now gives us many answers. We are not identical. Men and women should be equal in terms of their opportunities to exercise their full potential, but they are definitely not identical in their innate abilities. Whether men and women are *equal* is a political or moral question, but whether they are *identical* is a scientific one.

The equality of men and women is a political or moral issue; the essential difference is a scientific one.

Those who resist the idea that our biology affects our behaviour often do so with the best of intentions – they oppose sexism. But they are confused about the difference between *equal* and *identical* which are two completely different issues. In this book, you will see how science confirms that men and woman are profoundly different both physically and mentally. They are *not* the same.

We have investigated the research of leading palaeontologists, ethnologists, psychologists, biologists and neuroscientists. The brain differences between women and men are now clear, beyond all speculation, prejudice or reasonable doubt.

When weighing up the differences between males and females discussed in this book, some people may say, 'No, that's not like me, I don't do that!' Well, maybe they don't. But we are dealing here with *average* men and women, that is, how most men and women behave most of the time, in most situations and for most of the past. 'Average' means that if you are in a room full of people you'll notice that men are bigger and taller than women, in fact 7% taller and an average 8% bigger. The tallest or biggest person in the room may be a woman, but overall the men are bigger and taller than the women. In the *Guinness Book of World Records 2001*, the biggest and tallest people have almost always been men. The tallest human on record was Robert Wadlow from Alton, Illinois who, in June 1940, measured 2.72 metres (8 feet 11.1 inches). The tallest person in the year 2000 was Radhouane Charbib of Tunisia who stood 2.35 metres (7 feet 8.9 inches). History books are full of 'Big Johns' and 'Little Suzies'! This is not sexist. It's fact.

Where We (the Authors) Stand

Reading this book, some people may begin to feel smug, arrogant or angry. This is because, to a greater or lesser extent, they are victims of idealistic philosophies that claim women and men are the same, so let's clarify our position on this now. We, the authors, are writing this book to help you develop and improve your relationships with both sexes. We believe that men and women should have equal opportunity to pursue a career path in any field they choose and that equally qualified people should receive equal compensation for the same effort.

Difference is not the opposite of equality. Equality means being free to choose to do the things we want to do and difference means that, as men or women, we may not want to do the same things. We usually choose different things off the same list.

Our aim is to look objectively at male and female relationships, explain the history, meanings and implications involved and to develop techniques and strategies for a happier and more fulfilling way of life. We won't beat about the bush with suppositions, politically correct clichés or scientific mumbo-jumbo. If something looks like a duck, sounds like a duck, walks like a duck and there is enough evidence to prove it's a duck, then that's what we'll call it.

The evidence presented here shows that the sexes are intrinsically *inclined* to behave in different ways. We are not suggesting that either sex is bound to behave or should behave in any particular way.

The Nature Versus Nurture Argument

Melissa gave birth to twins, a girl and a boy. Jasmine, she wrapped in a pink blanket, and Adam, in a blue one. Relatives brought soft fluffy toys as gifts for Jasmine, and a toy football and a tiny football jersey for Adam. Everyone cooed and gooed and talked softly to Jasmine, telling her she was pretty and gorgeous, but it was usually only the female relatives who picked her up and cuddled her. When the male relatives visited, they focused mostly on Adam, speaking noticeably louder, poking his belly, bouncing him up and down and proposing a future as a football player.

Such a scenario will be familiar to everyone. It does, however, raise the question: Is this adult behaviour caused by our biology or is it learned behaviour that is perpetuated from generation to generation? Is it nature or nurture?

9

For most of the 20th century, psychologists and sociologists believed most of our behaviour and preferences were learnt from our social conditioning and our environment. However, we know that nurturing is a learned phenomenon – adoptive mothers, whether they are human or monkey, usually do a superb job of nurturing their infants. Scientists, on the other hand, have argued that biology, chemistry and hormones are largely responsible. Since 1990, there has been overwhelming evidence to support this scientific view that we are born with much of our brain software already in place. The fact that men were usually the hunters and women the nurturers even today dictates our behaviour, beliefs and priorities. A major study at Harvard University shows that we not only behave differently towards boy and girl babies, we also use different words. To baby girls we softly say, 'You're so sweet', 'You're a little sweetheart', 'You're a beautiful little girl' and to baby boys we raise our voices and say, 'Hey, big boy!' and 'Wow, you're so strong!'

Yet giving Barbie Dolls to girls and Action Men to boys does not create their behaviour; it simply exacerbates it. Similarly, the Harvard study found that adults' distinctive behaviour towards baby girls and boys only accentuated the differences that already exist. When you put a duck on a pond, it starts to swim. Look beneath the surface, and you'll see the duck has webbed feet. If you analyse its brain, you'll find that it evolved with a 'swimming module' already in place. The pond is just where the duck happens to be at the time and is not causing its behaviour.

Research shows that we are more a product of our biology than the victims of social stereotypes. We are different because our brain is wired differently. This causes us to perceive the world in different ways and have different values and priorities. Not better or worse – different.

Your Human Guidebook

This book is like a guidebook to visit a foreign culture or country. It contains local slang and phrases, body language signals and an insight into why the inhabitants are the way they are.

Most tourists travel to foreign countries without having done much local research and become intimidated or critical because the locals won't speak English or cook burgers and chips. But to enjoy and benefit from the experience of another culture you must first understand its history and evolution. Then you need to learn basic phrases and to sample their lifestyle for first hand experience and a deeper appreciation of that culture. That way you won't look, sound and act like a tourist – the kind of person who would have benefited just as much from staying at home and merely *thinking* of other lands.

This book will show you how to enjoy and benefit from the knowledge of the opposite sex. But first you must understand their history and evolution.

On a visit to Windsor Castle,

an American tourist was heard to say,

'It's a wonderful castle, but why did

they build it so close to the airport?'

This book deals in facts and reality. It's about real people, authentic research, actual events and recorded conversations. And you don't need to worry about dendrites, corpus callosum, neuropeptides, magnetic resonance imaging and serotonin in researching brain function. We did, but we're now keeping everything as simple as possible to make it easy to read. We deal largely with a relatively recent science called sociobiology – the study of how behaviour is explained by our genes and our evolution.

You will discover a powerful set of concepts, techniques and strategies that are scientifically substantiated and appear, for the most part, to be obvious or common sense. We've cast aside all techniques, practices or opinions that aren't grounded in, or proven by, science.

We deal here with the modern naked ape – the ape who controls the world with mega-computers and can land on Mars, and who can still be traced directly back to a fish. Millions of years was spent developing us as a species, yet today, we are thrust into a technological, politically correct world that makes little or no allowance for our biology.

It took us nearly 100 million years to evolve into a society sophisticated enough to put a man on the moon, but he still had to go to the toilet like his primitive ancestors when he got there. Humans may look a little different from one culture to another but, underneath, our biological needs and urges are the same. We will demonstrate how our different behavioural traits are inherited or passed on from generation to generation and, as you will see, there are practically no cultural differences.

Let's now take a brief look at how our brain evolved.

How We Got This Way

Once upon a time, a long, long time ago, men and women lived happily together and worked in harmony. The man would venture out each day into a hostile and dangerous world to risk his life as a hunter to bring food back to his woman and their children, and he would defend them against savage animals or enemies. He developed long-distance navigational skills so he could locate food and bring it home, and excellent marksmanship skills so that he could hit a moving target. His job description was straightforward: he was a lunch-chaser, and that's all anyone expected of him.

The woman, however, felt valued because her man would put his life on the line to care for his family. His success as a man was measured by his ability to make a kill and bring it home, and his self-worth was measured by her appreciation for his struggle and effort. The family depended on him to carry out his job description as a lunch-chaser and protector – and nothing else. There was never any need for him to 'analyse the relationship' and he wasn't expected to put out the garbage or help change the nappies.

The woman's role was equally clear. Being appointed the child-bearer directed the way she would evolve and how her skills would become specialised to meet that role. She needed to be able to monitor her immediate surroundings for signs of danger, have excellent short-range navigational skills, using landmarks to find her way, and have a highly-tuned ability to sense small changes in the behaviour and appearance of children and adults. Things were simple: He was the lunch-chaser, she was the nest-defender.

Her day would be spent caring for her children, collecting fruits, vegetables and nuts and interacting with the other women in the group. She did not have to concern herself with the major food supply or fighting enemies, and her success was measured by her ability to sustain family life. Her self-worth came from the man's appreciation of her home-making and nurturing skills. Her ability to bear children was considered magical, even sacred, for she alone held the secret to giving life. She was never expected to hunt animals, fight enemies or change light bulbs.

Survival was difficult but the relationship was easy. And this was the way it was for hundreds of thousands of years. At the end of each day, the hunters would return with their kill. The kill was divided equally and everyone would eat together in the communal cave. Each hunter would trade part of his kill with the woman for her fruit and vegetables.

After the meal, the men would sit around the fire, gazing into it, playing games, telling stories or sharing jokes. It was a prehistoric man's version of flicking TV channels with his remote control or being absorbed in a newspaper. They were exhausted from their hunting efforts and were recuperating to begin the hunt again the next day. The women would continue to tend the children and make sure the men were sufficiently fed and rested. Each appreciated the other's efforts. Men were not considered lazy and women were not seen as their oppressed handmaidens.

These simple rituals and behaviours still exist amongst ancient civilisations in places like Borneo, parts of Africa and Indonesia, and with some Aboriginal Australians, New Zealand Maoris, and the Inuit of Canada and Greenland. In these cultures each person knows and understands his or her role. Men appreciate women and women appreciate men. Each sees the other as uniquely contributing to the family's survival and well-being. But for men and women who live in modern civilised countries, these old rules have been thrown out – and chaos, confusion and unhappiness have been left in their place.

We Didn't Expect it to Be Like This

The family unit is no longer solely dependent on men for its survival and women are no longer expected to stay at home as nurturers and home-makers. For the first time in the history of our species, most men and women are confused about their job descriptions. You, the reader of this book, are the first generation of humans to face a set of circumstances that your forefathers or mothers never had to tackle. For the first time ever, we are looking to our partners for love, passion and personal fulfilment because basic survival is no longer critical. Our modern social structure usually provides a basic level of subsistence through social security, National Health, consumer protection laws and various Government institutions. So what are the new rules, and where do you learn them? This book attempts to provide some answers.

Why Mum and Dad Can't Help

If you were born before 1960, you grew up watching your parents behave towards each other based on the ancient rules of male and female survival. Your parents were repeating the behaviour they learned from *their* parents who, in turn, were copying *their* parents, who mimicked *their* parents, and back it goes to the ancient cave people in their clearly defined roles.

Now the rules have changed completely, and your parents don't know how to help. The divorce rate for newlyweds is now around 50% and, taking defacto and gay relationships into consideration, the *real* breakup rate for couples is likely to be over 70%. We need to learn a new set of rules in order to discover how to be happy and survive emotionally intact into the 21st Century.

We're Still Just Another Animal

Most people have difficulty thinking of themselves as just another animal. They refuse to face the fact that 96% of what can be found in their bodies can also be found inside a pig or a horse or that our DNA is 97.5% identical to that of a gorilla and 98.4% to that of a chimpanzee. The only thing that makes us different from other animals is our ability to think and make forward plans. Other animals can only respond to situations based on the genetic wiring of their brain and by repetition of behaviour. They cannot think; they can only react.

Most people accept and acknowledge that animals have instincts that largely determine their behaviour. This instinctive behaviour is easy to see – birds sing, frogs croak, male dogs cock their leg and cats stalk their prey. But these are not intellectual behaviours, so many people have difficulty making the connection between this behaviour and their own. They even ignore the fact that their own first behaviours were instinctive – crying and sucking.

Whatever behaviours we inherit, positive or negative, from our parents are likely to be passed on to our children the same way it happens with all animals. When we as humans accept ourselves as an animal whose impulses are honed by millions of years of evolution, it makes it easier to understand our basic urges and impulses, and to be more accepting of ourselves and others. And therein lies the way to true happiness.

CHAPTER 2
MAKING PERFECT SENSE

Men can never find things ...

The party was already in full swing when John and Sue arrived. Inside, Sue looked John full in the face and, without appearing to move her lips, said, 'Look at that couple over by the window.' John turned his head to take a look. 'Don't look now!' she hissed, 'you're so obvious!' Sue couldn't understand why John had to turn his head so indiscreetly, and John couldn't believe that Sue could see the other people in the room without doing so.

In this chapter we will explore research into the sensory perception differences between men and women and the implications they have on our relationships.

Women as Radar Detectors

It is obvious to a woman when another woman is upset or feeling hurt, while a man would generally have to physically witness tears, a temper tantrum or be slapped around the face before he'd even have a clue anything was going on. For, like most female mammals, women are equipped with far more finely tuned sensory skills than men. As child-bearers and nest-defenders, they needed the ability to sense subtle mood and attitude changes in others. What is commonly called 'women's intuition' is mostly a woman's acute ability to notice small details and changes in the appearance or behaviour of others. It's something that, throughout history, has bewildered men who play around – and are invariably caught.

One of our friends said he couldn't believe how wonderful his wife's eyesight was when he had something to hide, but how it seemed to desert her totally when it came to backing the car into the garage. Estimating the distance between the car fender and the garage wall while moving is, however, a spatial skill located in the right hemisphere in men and is not strong in most women. We'll discuss that later in Chapter 5.

> *'My wife can see a blonde hair on my coat from twenty feet, but she hits the garage door when she parks the car.'*

Nest-defenders, to safeguard their family's survival, needed to be able to pick up small changes in the behaviour of their offspring that could signal pain, hunger, injury, aggression or depression. Males, being lunch-chasers, were never around the cave long enough to learn to read non-verbal signals or the ways of interpersonal communication. Neuropsychologist Professor Ruben Gur of the University of Pennsylvania used brain scan tests to show that when a man's brain is in a resting state, at least 70% of its electrical activity is shut down. Scans of women's brains showed 90% activity during the same state, confirming that women are constantly receiving and analysing information from their environment. A woman knows her children's friends, hopes, dreams, romances, secret fears, what they are thinking, how they are feeling and, usually, what mischief they are plotting. Men are vaguely aware of some short people also living in the house.

The Eyes Have It

The eye is an extension of the brain that sits outside the skull. The retina at the back of the eyeball contains about

130 million rod-shaped cells called photoreceptors to deal with black and white, and seven million cone-shaped cells to handle colour. The X chromosome provides these colour cells. Women have two X chromosomes which gives them a greater variety of cones than men and this difference is noticeable in how women describe colours in greater detail. A man will use basic colour descriptions like red, blue and green, but a woman will talk of bone, aqua, teal, mauve and apple green.

Human eyes have noticeable whites which other primates lack. This allows for the movement of the eye and the direction of the gaze which are vital to human face-to-face communication. Women's eyes display more white than men's eyes because close-range personal communication is an integral part of female bonding, and more white allows a greater range of eye signals to be sent and received in the direction that the eyes move.

This type of eye communication is not critical to most other species of animal and so they have little or no whites and rely on body language as the main form of communication.

Eyes in the Back of her Head?

Well, not quite, but close. Women not only have a greater variety of concs in the retina, they also have wider peripheral vision than men. As a nest-defender, a woman has brain software that allows her to receive an arc of at least 45° clear vision to each side of her head and above and below her nose. Many women's peripheral vision is effective up to almost 180°. A man's eyes are larger than a woman's and his brain configures them for a type of long-distance tunnel vision which means that he can see clearly and accurately directly in front of him and over greater distances, almost like a pair of binoculars.

Women have wider peripheral vision, men have tunnel vision.

As a hunter, a man needed vision that would allow him to zero in on, and pursue, targets in the distance. He evolved with almost blinkered vision so that he would not be distracted from targets, whereas a woman needed eyes to allow a wide arc of vision so that she could monitor any predators sneaking up on the nest. This is why modern men can find their way effortlessly to a distant pub, but can never find things in fridges, cupboards and drawers.

In the UK in 1997, there were 4,132 child pedestrians killed or injured on the roads, of which 2,640 were boys and 1,492 were girls. In Australia, boy pedestrian fatalities and injuries are more than double that of girls. Boys take more risks crossing the road than girls and this, combined with poorer peripheral vision, increases their injury rate.

The range of vision for male and female eyes

You can increase your peripheral vision range with practice, just as fighter pilots do. The arc of a person's peripheral vision can also increase under life-threatening circumstances. During a prison riot at Australia's Perth prison in 1999, inmates held several prison officers hostage. They announced that unless their demands were met, the officers would be killed. Prison officer Lance Bremen reported that, until that time, he had 'typical male tunnel vision'. Having survived the incident, his peripheral vision had increased to almost 180 degrees. Because of the trauma of the event and the fear of being killed, his brain had expanded his vision range to monitor anyone trying to sneak up on him.

Why Women's Eyes See So Much

Billions of photons of light equal to 100 megabytes of computer data strike the retina of the eye every second. This is too much for the brain to handle so it edits the information down to only what is necessary for survival. For example, once your brain understands all the colours of the sky, it selects only what it needs to see – the colour blue. Our brain narrows our vision so that we can concentrate on a specific thing. If we are searching for a needle in a carpet, we have a more concentrated narrow field of vision. Men's brains, being pre-wired for hunting, see a much narrower field. Women's brains decode information over a wider peripheral range because of their past defending the nest.

The Slippery Case of the Missing Butter

Every woman in the world has had the following conversation with a male who is standing in front of an open fridge.

> *David:* 'Where's the butter?'
> *Jan:* 'It's in the fridge.'
> *David:* 'I'm looking there, but I can't see any butter.'
> *Jan:* 'Well it's there. I put it in ten minutes ago!'
> *David:* 'No. You must have put it somewhere else. There's definitely no butter in this fridge!'

At that, Jan strides into the kitchen, thrusts her arm into the fridge and, as if by magic, produces a tub of butter. Inexperienced men sometimes feel that this is a trick and they accuse women of always hiding things from them in drawers and cupboards. Socks, shoes, underwear, jam, butter, car keys, wallets – they're all there, they just can't see them. With her wider arc of peripheral vision a woman can see most of the contents of a fridge or cupboard without moving her head. Her oestrogen hormones allow her to identify matching items in a drawer, cupboard or across a room and later remember objects in a complex random pattern – such as where the butter or jam is in the refrigerator. New research also suggests that male brains are searching in the fridge for the word B-U-T-T-E-R. If it's facing the wrong way, he virtually can't see it. This is why men move their heads. Men move their heads from side to side and up and down as they scan for the 'missing' objects.

These differences in vision have important implications throughout our lives. Car insurance statistics, for instance, show female drivers are less likely to be hit from the side in an accident at an intersection than male drivers. Women's greater peripheral vision allows them to see traffic approaching from the side. They are more likely to be hit in the front or back of the car while attempting to reverse parallel park, as that challenges their less-developed spatial skills.

A woman's life is much less stressful when she understands the problems men have seeing things at close range.

When a woman tells a man, 'It's in the cupboard!' it is less stressful for him to believe her and continue the search.

Men and Ogling

Wider peripheral vision is the reason why women rarely get caught ogling men.

Almost every man has been accused at some time or other of ogling the opposite sex, but few women receive the same complaint from men. Sex researchers everywhere report that women look at men's bodies as much as, and sometimes more than, men look at women's. Yet women, with their superior peripheral vision, rarely get caught.

Seeing is Believing

Most people won't believe something until they see the proof – but can you trust your eyes? Millions believe in UFOs despite the fact that 92% of all UFO sightings are in remote country areas on Saturday nights around eleven o'clock – just after the pubs close. There has never been a UFO sighting by a Prime Minister or President and UFOs never land on a University Campus, Government research laboratory or Parliament. And they never land in bad weather.

Researcher Edward Boring devised the following illustration to show how we each perceive different things in the same picture. Women are more likely to see an old woman with her chin tucked into the collar of her fur coat but men are more likely to see the left-side profile of a young woman who is looking away.

The picture of the table also shows that what you see is not necessarily what you get.

Your brain is fooled into believing that the far side of the table is longer than the front side. Women are usually amused by this, but men demand proof and grab a ruler to measure it.

In the picture above your brain focuses on the solid colour so it looks like a group of odd shapes. When you change the way you look at it and concentrate on the white portions the word FLY will appear. A woman is more likely to see FLY than a man as his brain gets stuck on the geometric shapes.

Why Men Should Drive at Night

While a woman can see better in the dark than a man, especially at the red end of the spectrum, a man's eyes allow for better long-distance vision over a narrower field, which gives him much better – and therefore safer – long-distance night vision than a woman. Combined with his right brain spatial ability, a man can separate and identify the movement of other vehicles on the road ahead and behind. Most women can testify to what is a kind of night blindness: the inability to distinguish which side of the road approaching traffic is on. This is a task that a man's hunting vision is equipped to handle. This means that if you are going on a long driving trip, it makes sense for a woman to drive during the day and for a man to drive at night. Women can see more detail in the dark than men but only over a shorter, wider field.

On long trips, men should drive at

night and women drive in the day.

Men suffer greater eyestrain than women because their eyes are configured for long distances and must be constantly readjusted to look at a computer screen or read a newspaper. A woman's eyes are better suited for close-range activities, giving her a longer working time on fine detail. In addition, her brain is wired for coordinated fine-motor capability in a small area, which means the average woman is excellent at threading a needle and reading detail on a computer screen.

Why Women Have a 'Sixth Sense'

For centuries women were burned at the stake for possessing 'supernatural powers'. These included the ability to predict outcomes of relationships, spot liars, talk to animals and uncover the truth.

In 1978, we conducted an experiment for a television programme which highlighted women's ability to read the body language signals of babies. At a maternity hospital, we collated a selection of ten-second film clips of crying babies and asked the mothers to watch the clips with the sound turned down. This way the mothers received only visual information.

Most mothers could quickly detect a range of emotions ranging from hunger and pain to wind or tiredness. When the fathers did the same test, their success rate was pitiful – fewer than 10% of fathers could pick more than two emotions. Even then, we suspect many were probably guessing. Many fathers would triumphantly announce, 'The baby wants its mother.' Most men had little, if any, ability to decode the differences in baby cries. We also tested the grandparents to see if age affected the outcome. Most grandmothers scored 50–70% of the mother's score, while many grandfathers could not even identify their own grandchild!

Our study with identical twins revealed that most grandfathers were unable to identify each twin individually, whereas most female family members had less difficulty with this task. In a room of fifty couples it takes the average woman less than ten minutes to analyse the relationship between each couple in the room. When a woman enters a room, her superior sensory abilities enable her to rapidly identify couples who are getting on with each other, who's had an argument, who is making advances on whom and where the competitive or friendly women are. When a man enters a room, our cameras show a different story. Men scan the room looking for exits and entries – his ancient brain-wiring evaluates where a potential attack may come from and possible escape routes. Next, he looks for familiar faces or possible enemies and then scans the room layout. His logical mind will register things that need to be fixed or repaired such as broken windows or a blown light bulb. Meanwhile, the women have scanned all the faces in the room and know what's what, who's who and how they are all feeling.

Why Men Can't Lie to Women

Our Body Language research reveals that, in face-to-face communications, non-verbal signals account for 60–80% of the impact of the message, while vocal sounds make up 20–30%. The other 7–10% is words. A woman's superior sensory equipment picks up and analyses this information and her brain's ability to rapidly transfer between hemispheres makes her more proficient at integrating and deciphering verbal, visual and other signals.

This is why most men have difficulty lying to a woman face-to-face. But, as most women know, lying to a man face-to-face is comparatively easy, as he does not have the necessary sensitivity to spot incongruencies between her verbal and non-verbal signals. Most men, if they're going to lie to a woman, would be far better off doing it over the phone, in a letter or with all the lights off, and a blanket over their heads.

She Hears Better Too ...

Women hear better than men and are excellent at distinguishing high-pitched sounds. A woman's brain is programmed to hear a baby cry in the night, whereas a father may be oblivious to it and sleep on. If there is a kitten crying in the distance, a woman will hear it. A man, however, with his superior spatial and directional skills, can tell her where it is.

Dripping taps drive women

crazy, while men sleep.

At one week, baby girls can distinguish their mother's voice or the cry of another baby from the other sounds that are present in the same room. Baby boys can't. Males use their left brain only for listening but females use both brains for this task. The female brain has the ability to separate and categorise sound and make decisions about each sound. This accounts for a woman's ability to listen to one person in a face-to-face conversation while monitoring another person's conversation. It also explains why a man has difficulty hearing a conversation while there is a television on in the background or dishes are being clattered in the sink. If a phone rings, a man will demand people stop talking, music is turned down and the TV is switched off for him to answer it. A woman simply answers the phone.

Women Read Between the Lines

Women have superior sensitivity in differentiating tone changes in voice volume and pitch. This enables them to hear emotional changes in children and adults. Consequently, for every man who can sing in tune, there are eight women who can do it. This ability goes a long way to explaining the women's phrase, 'Don't use that tone of voice with me!' when arguing with men and boys. Most males don't have a clue what she's talking about.

Tests conducted on babies reveal that baby girls respond almost twice as much to a loud sound than boys. This explains why girls are more easily soothed and comforted by high-pitched baby talk than boys, and why mothers intuitively sing lullabies to girls, but talk to, or play with, boys. Female hearing advantage contributes significantly to what is called 'Women's Intuition' and is one of the reasons why a woman can read between the lines of what people say. Men, however, shouldn't despair. They are excellent at identifying and imitating animal sounds, which would have been a significant advantage for the ancient hunter. Sadly, that's not quite as much use today.

Men Can 'Hear' Direction

Women are better at differentiating sounds but men can point to where they're coming from. Combined with the male ability to identify and imitate animal sounds, this skill makes him a highly efficient hunter of game. So how does sound get converted in the brain into a map?

Professor Masakazu Konishi of the California Institute of Technology discovered some of the answers using barn owls, birds that are better than humans at pinpointing where a sound is coming from. Play them a sound and they will turn their heads to face its source. Konishi discovered a group of cells in the auditory region of their brains that mapped the exact location of a sound. Speakers that played the same sound to each of the owls' ears at a different rate of speed – about 200 millionths of a second – allowed the owls' brains to form a 3D spatial map of the sound's location. The owls then turned their heads towards the sound, allowing them to locate prey or avoid approaching enemies. This appears to be the same ability that men use to pinpoint sound.

Why Boys Don't Listen

Boys are often chastised by their teachers and parents for not listening. But as boys grow, particularly approaching puberty, their ear canals undergo growth spurts that can cause a temporary form of deafness. Female teachers have been found to reprimand girls differently to boys and seem intuitively to understand male and female hearing differences.

If a girl refuses to keep eye contact while the teacher berates her, a female teacher will continue the reprimand. If a boy refuses eye contact, many female teachers intuitively understand that he probably either can't hear or is not listening, and will say, 'Look at me when I speak to you'. Unfortunately, boys are equipped for effective seeing rather than hearing. For an easy demonstration of this, just count the number of *Fs* in the following sentence.

Finished files are the result of

years of scientific research.

Boys score better than girls at seeing that there are five *F's*. If the statement is read aloud however, girls are better than boys at hearing the correct number of *F's*.

Men Miss the Details

Lyn and Chris are driving home from a party. He's driving, she's navigating and they've just had an argument about her telling him to turn left when she really meant right. Nine minutes of silence has passed and he suspects something is up. 'Darling ... is everything OK?' asks Chris. 'Yes – everything's *fine!*" Lyn answers.

Her emphasis on the word 'fine' confirms that things are actually far from fine. He thinks back to the party. 'Did I do something wrong tonight?' asks Chris. 'I don't want to talk about it!' she snaps.

This means she's angry and *does* want to talk about it. Meanwhile, he's at a complete loss to understand what he's done to upset her. 'Please tell me. What did I do?' he pleads. 'I don't know what I did!'

In most conversations like this one, the man is telling the truth – he simply doesn't understand the problem. 'OK then,' she says, 'I'll tell you the problem even though you're playing that stupid act!' But it's not an act. He genuinely doesn't have a handle on the problem. She takes a deep breath. 'That bimbo was hanging around you all night giving you come-on signals and you didn't get rid of her – you encouraged her!'

Now Chris is completely dumbstruck. What bimbo? What come-on signals? He didn't see anything. You see, while the 'bimbo' (this is a woman's expression; men would describe a woman like that as 'sexy') had been talking to him, he hadn't noticed that she was tilting her pelvis at him, pointing her foot his way, flicking her hair, stroking her thigh, massaging her earlobes, giving him longer than usual glances, stroking the stem of her wine glass and talking like a schoolgirl. He's a hunter. He can spot a zebra on the horizon and tell you how fast it's moving. He doesn't have a woman's ability to pick up the visual, vocal and body language signals that say someone's on the make. Every woman at the party saw what the 'bimbo' was doing even without moving their heads. And a telepathic 'bitch alert' was sent and received by all other women at the party. Most of the men missed it completely.

So when a man claims he is telling the truth about these accusations, he probably is. Male brains are not equipped to hear or see details.

The Magic of Touch

Touch can be life-giving. Early tests conducted on monkeys by Harlow and Zimmerman showed that lack of touch on infant monkeys resulted in depression, illness and premature death. Similar results have been found in neglected children. An impressive study on babies from ten weeks of age to six months, found that the offspring of mothers who were taught to stroke their babies had dramatically fewer colds and sniffles, and less vomiting and diarrhoea than those whose mothers didn't stroke them. Other research found that women who were neurotic or depressed recovered much more quickly according to the number of times they were hugged, and the duration of those hugs.

Anthropologist James Prescott, who pioneered the study of child-rearing and violence, found that societies in which children were rarely touched affectionately, had the highest rates of adult violence. Children brought up with affectionate carers usually ended up growing into better, healthier and happier adults. Sex offenders and child molesters both tended to have pasts characterised by rejection, violence, a lack of cuddles as children, and childhoods, often, spent in remote institutions. Many non-touching cultures love cats and dogs as they allow them to experience touch via stroking and patting their pets. Pet-patting therapy has proved to be a valuable way of helping people overcome depression and other mental problems. Just look at how the English, the very antipathy of a touchy-feely race, love their pets. As Germaine Greer said, 'Even crushed against his brother in the Tube the average Englishman pretends desperately that he is alone.'

Women Are Touchy-Feely

The skin is the largest organ in the body, measuring around two square metres. Distributed unevenly across it are 2,800,000 receptors for pain, 200,000 for cold, and 500,000 for touch and pressure. From birth, girls are dramatically more sensitive to touch and, as an adult, a woman's skin is at least ten times more sensitive to touch and pressure than a man's. In one authoritative study it was found that the boys who tested most sensitive to touch felt even less than the least sensitive girls. Female skin is thinner than male skin and has an extra fat layer below it for more warmth in winter and to provide greater endurance.

Oxytocin is the hormone that stimulates the urge to be touched and fires up our touch receptors. It's no wonder that women, with receptors that are ten times more sensitive than men's, attach so much importance to cuddling their men, children and friends. Our body language research shows that western women are four to six times more likely to touch another woman in a social conversation than a man is likely to touch another man. Women use a greater range of touch expressions than men, describing a successful person as having a 'magic touch' and others as being 'thin-skinned' or 'thick-skinned'. Women love 'staying in touch' and dislike those who 'get under your skin'. They talk about 'feelings', giving someone 'the personal touch', being 'touchy' and annoying people by 'rubbing them up the wrong way'. In 1999, a research team led by Michael Meaney at McGill University in Quebec, Canada, showed baby rats that are constantly groomed and cared for by their parents develop more brain mass and higher intelligence than baby rats who had less caring parents.

A study with psychiatric patients showed that, under pressure, men avoid touch and retreat into their own world. More than half the women in the same test, on the other hand, initiated approaches to men, not for sex, but for the intimacy of touch. When a woman is emotionally cut off or angry with a man, she is likely to respond by saying, 'Don't touch me!', a phrase that has little meaning to men. The lesson? To win points with women, use lots of appropriate touching but avoid groping. To raise mentally healthy children, cuddle them a lot.

> *A woman is four to six times*
>
> *more likely to touch another*
>
> *woman in a social conversation*
>
> *than a man would another man.*

Why Men Are So Thick-Skinned

Men have thicker skin than women which explains why women get more wrinkles than men. The skin on a man's back is four times thicker than his stomach skin, a legacy from his four-legged animal past which gave more protection from a rear attack. Most of a boy's sensitivity to touch is lost by the time he reaches puberty and his body prepares itself for the rigours of the hunt. Males needed desensitised skin to run through prickly bushes, wrestle animals and fight enemies without the pain slowing them down. When a man is focused on a physical task or sporting activity, he is unlikely even to be aware of injury.

> *A boy doesn't really lose skin sensitivity*
>
> *at puberty, it just all goes to one area.*

When a man is not focused on a task, his threshold of pain is much lower than a woman's. When a man moans, 'Make me some chicken soup/fresh orange juice/get me a hot water bottle/call the doctor, and make sure my Will is in order!', it usually means he's got a slight head cold. Men are also less sensitive to a woman who is suffering pain or discomfort. If she's doubled up in pain, has a temperature of 104 degrees and is shivering under the blankets he says, 'Is everything OK darling?' but he's thinking, 'If I ignore it, maybe she'll have sex – she's in bed anyway.'

Men do feel sensitivity when watching football or aggressive sports, however. If men are watching a boxing match on TV and one of the boxers is felled by a low blow a woman will say, 'Oooh ... that must have hurt' while the men all groan, double over and actually *feel* the pain.

A Taste for Life

Women's senses of taste and smell are superior to men's. We have up to 10,000 taste receptors to detect at least four major tastes; sweet and salt on the tip of the tongue, sour on the sides and bitter at the back. Japanese researchers are currently testing a fifth taste – the taste of fat. Men score higher on discerning salty and bitter tastes which is why they drink beer, and women are far superior in discerning sweet and sugar tastes, which is why there are far more female chocoholics in the world than male. As the nest-defender and fruit-gatherer, tasting foods to check they were sweet and ripe enough to pass on to her brood, it was an advantage to have a highly refined sugar-tasting palate. This explains why women love sugary sweets and why most food tasters are women.

Something in the Air

Not only is a woman's sense of smell better than the average man's, it is even more sensitive around the ovulation stage of her monthly cycle. Her nose can detect the pheromones and musk-like odours associated with men and these are scents that cannot be detected consciously. Her brain is able to decode the state of a man's immune system and, if it's complementary to, or stronger than her own immune system, she may describe a man as attractive or 'strangely magnetic'. If her immune system is stronger than his, she is likely to find him less attractive.

Brain researchers have discovered that a woman's brain can analyse these immune system differences within three seconds of a meeting. Complementary immune systems pass on an advantage to offspring by giving them a greater chance of survival. One outcome of all this research has been the number of oils and potions now being marketed for men that supposedly contain the secret of surefire pheromone attraction, driving women wild with desire.

A strong immune system can make

a man seem 'strangely compelling'.

The X-Philes

Our evolutionary roles have equipped us with the biological skills and senses we need for survival. What is often called witchcraft, supernatural power and women's intuition has been scientifically tested and measured since the 1980s and, for the most part, comes down to a woman's superiority in all the perceptive senses. Most witches were women who were put to death by men who could not understand the biological differences. Women are simply better at picking up the small nuances in body language, vocal cues, tone of voice and other sensory stimuli. They can also read attitudes and emotions in animals. This allowed ancient women to determine whether or not an animal approaching her nest was dangerous or friendly. A woman can even tell if a dog is feeling embarrassed or if a horse is about to kick. Most men cannot imagine what an embarrassed dog looks like. Women counsel cats. When women are not looking, men kick cats.

For nest-defending women, being dextrous with both hands would have been an advantage to the process of gathering as it gives twice the speed. Consequently, many women do not have a specific area in either brain for identifying left from right – it was never necessary. This is why there are disproportionately more ambidextrous women than men. It also explains why women everywhere are unfairly criticised by men who, frustrated at being given wrong directions by a woman, yell, 'Don't you even know your left from right!' The correct answer is 'no'– a dominant right hand is vital to target-hitting, but not critical to fast gathering. Because of their superior abilities in this area, modern women are still victimised by their attraction to astrologers, psychics, tarot card readers, numerologists and others who offer an explanation for female intuition in exchange for hard-earned money. A woman's highly refined sensors contribute significantly to the early maturity of adolescent girls. By the age of seventeen, most girls can function as adults, while the boys are still giving each other wedgies at the swimming pool and lighting farts.

Why Men Are Called 'Insensitive'

It's not so much that women have super senses – it's more that men's senses have been dulled, comparatively speaking. In a woman's world of higher perceptiveness, she expects a man to read her verbal, vocal and body language signals and to anticipate her needs, just as another woman would do. For the evolutionary reasons discussed, this simply is not the case. A woman quietly assumes that a man will know what she wants or needs and, when he doesn't pick up on her cues, she accuses him of being, 'Insensitive – wouldn't have a clue!' Men everywhere bleat, 'Am I supposed to be a mindreader?' Research proves that men are poor mindreaders. But the good news is that most can be trained to improve their awareness of non-verbal and vocal messages.

The next chapter has a unique test that will show you the sexual orientation of your brain and why you are the way you are.

CHAPTER 3
IT'S ALL IN THE MIND

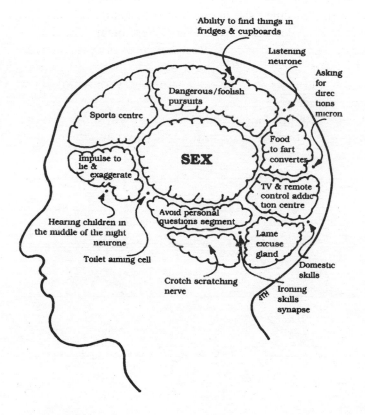

The male brain

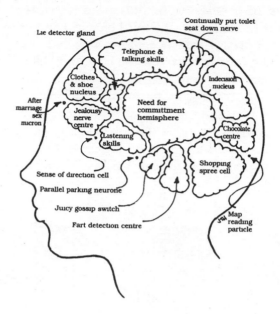

The female brain

These lighthearted illustrations of the male and female brain are funny only because they contain such an element of truth. But how much? Well, more than you might think. In this chapter we'll examine the recent dramatic revelations from research into the brain.

You'll find this chapter a real eye-opener, and at the end we have included a simple but remarkable test to show you just why your brain behaves the way it does.

Why We're Smarter than the Rest

Look at the following drawings and you'll notice two striking differences between gorillas, Neanderthal man and us modern humans. Firstly, our brain is more than three times the size of the gorilla's and one-third bigger than our primitive ancestor's. Fossil evidence shows that our brain has remained about the same size for the last 50,000 years and there has been little change in our brain functions. Secondly, we have a protruding forehead which our forefathers and primate cousins lacked. The forehead contains the left and right frontal brain lobes which give us many of our unique abilities such as thinking, map reading and speech. This is what makes us superior to all other animals.

gorilla   Neanderthal man   modern man

Men and women's brains have evolved with different strengths, talents and abilities. Men, being responsible for hunting game, needed areas in the brain for long-distance navigation, to develop tactics for organising the kill and to hone skills for hitting a target. They didn't need to be good conversationalists or sensitive to anyone's emotional needs, so they never developed strong brain areas for interpersonal skills.

Women, by contrast, needed an aptitude for good short-range navigation, wider peripheral vision to monitor their surroundings, the ability to perform several activities simultaneously, and effective communication skills. As a consequence of these needs, men and women's brains developed specific areas to handle each skill.

In today's terms, ancient society was very sexist but we'll tackle this issue later.

How Our Brains Defend Territory

'Old habits die hard,' say the old folks. 'Genetic memory is alive and operating,' say the scientists. Genetic memory is part of our instinctive behaviour. Naturally, you'd expect tens of thousands of years sitting in a cave facing outwards to monitor surroundings, defend territory and solve the myriad problems of survival, to leave quite a mark on men.

Just look at them in a restaurant. Most men prefer to sit with their backs to the wall, facing the restaurant entrance. This makes them feel comfortable, secure and alert. No one's going to sneak up on them unobserved, even if it is, these days, with nothing more lethal than a particularly hefty bill. Women, on the other hand, don't mind having their backs to an open space, unless they are alone with young children, when they'll tend to take a seat next to the wall.

At home, men will also act instinctively, by taking the side of the bed closest to the bedroom door – the symbolic act of defending the cave entrance. If a couple moves to a new home or stays in a hotel where the door is on the woman's side of the bed, a man can feel restless and may have difficulty sleeping without ever knowing why. Changing places so that he is once again closest to the door can often solve the problem.

Men joke that they sleep by the door of their first marital home for a quick get-away. In truth, it's pure defender instinct.

When a man is away from home, a woman will generally assume his protective role and sleep on his side of the bed. At night, a woman can be aroused from a deep sleep immediately by a high-pitched sound, like a baby's cry. Men, to women's great annoyance, will snore on soundly. But his brain is wired to hear sounds associated with movement and even the sound of a twig breaking outside his window can bring him wide awake in a split second to defend against a possible attack. This time, women will sleep on – except when the man is away and her brain becomes programmed to assume his role, and hear every sound or movement threatening the nest.

The Brains Behind Success

The Greek philosopher Aristotle believed that the centre for thought lay in the heart while the brain helped cool the body. This is why the heart is the object of many of our expressions of emotion. It may seem ridiculous to us now, but many experts, as recently as the late 19th Century, still agreed with Aristotle.

In 1962 Roger Sperry won a Nobel Prize for identifying that the two hemispheres of the brain's cerebral cortex are responsible for separate intellectual functions. Advanced technology is now allowing us to see how the brain operates, but our real understanding of brain function is still very basic. We know that the right hemisphere, which is the creative side, controls the left side of the body, while the left hemisphere controls logic, reason, speech and the body's right side. The left brain is where language and vocabulary are located, particularly for men, and the right brain stores and controls visual information.

People who are left-handed have a bias towards the right hemisphere, which is the creative side of the brain. It is for this reason that there is such a disproportionate number of left-handers who are artistic geniuses, including Albert Einstein, Leonardo Da Vinci, Picasso, Lewis Carroll, Greta Garbo, Robert De Niro and Paul McCartney. There are more left-handed women than men and 90% of all people are right-handed. Most men are very capable with their right arm and hand but are not as good with their left. For males, the right arm needs to be accurate at throwing objects at a moving target and to defend the front of the body from attack. This right-handedness for men appears to be located somewhere in the genes and explains why, if a man is going to attack, more than 90% of the time his first move will be a right side, over-arm blow.

Tests show that women rate three percent higher in general intelligence than men.

Until the 1960s, most of the data collected on the human brain came from soldiers killed on the battlefields – and there were plenty of candidates to work on. The problem was, however, that most of these were males and the silent assumption was that female brains operated in the same way.

Today, latest research reveals that the female brain operates significantly differently to the male brain. Therein lies the source of most of the problems in relationships between the sexes. The female brain is slightly smaller than the male brain but studies show this to have no significance on a woman's brain performance. In 1997 Danish researcher Bente Pakkenberg of the Neurology Department of Copenhagen Municipal Hospital demonstrated that, on average, a man has around four billion more brain cells than a woman but, generally, women test around 3% higher in general intelligence than men. In 1999, brain researcher Professor Ruben Gur of the University of

Pennsylvania Medical Centre discovered that women have more grey matter than men. Grey matter is where the brain does its computational work and makes women better communicators than men.

> *'It's obvious that women are smarter than men. Think about it – diamonds are a girl's best friend; man's best friend is a dog.'*
>
> Joan Rivers

What's Where in the Brain?

Here is a commonly held view of which side of the brain controls which function.

While research and our understanding of the human brain is increasing dramatically every day, there are varying interpretations of the research results. But there are several areas on which scientists and researchers do agree. Using Magnetic Resonance Imaging (MRI), which measures electrical activity in the brain, it is now possible to identify and measure the exact location of many specific functions in the brain. With brain-scanning equipment, we can see which part of the brain is handling a particular task. When a brain scan shows a specific location for a skill or function, it means that the person will usually be good at performing that skill, that they enjoy doing it and are attracted to occupations and pursuits that allow them to use it.

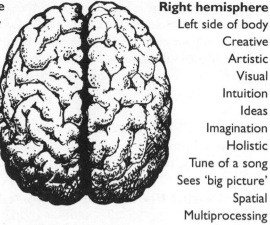

Left hemisphere	Right hemisphere
Right side of body	Left side of body
Mathematics	Creative
Verbal	Artistic
Logical	Visual
Facts	Intuition
Deduction	Ideas
Analysis	Imagination
Practical	Holistic
Order	Tune of a song
Words of a song	Sees 'big picture'
Lineal	Spatial
Sees fine detail	Multiprocessing

For example, most men have a specific brain location for sensing direction so they find that easy to do. They enjoy planning directions and are drawn to pursuits and pastimes that allow them to use abilities such as navigation and orientation. Women have specific areas for speech. They're good at it, can do it with ease and are attracted to fields that allow them to make use of this strength, such as therapy, counselling and teaching. Where there is no clear brain location for a certain skill it usually means that a person is not naturally good at, or does not particularly enjoy, tasks that make use of that skill. This is why it's as hard to locate female navigators as it is to find solace in a male counsellor, or learn 'proper' English from a male language teacher.

Where Brain Research Began

The first recorded scientific tests into differences between the sexes were held at the Museum of London by Francis Galton in 1882. He found that men had better sensitivity to 'bright' sounds – shrill or high-pitched noises – had a stronger hand grip and were less sensitive to pain than women. At the same time, in America, a similar study found that men preferred red to blue, had a larger vocabulary and preferred solving technical problems to domestic ones. Women could hear more acutely, used more words than men and preferred working on individual tasks and problems.

Early research into the specific location of brain functions came from brain-damaged patients. It was found that men who suffered injury to the left side of the brain had lost much or all of their speech and vocabulary skills, whereas women who were similarly brain-damaged did not suffer speech loss to the same extent, indicating that women have more than one centre for speech.

Men were three to four times more likely to suffer speech losses or speech impediments than women, and were much less likely to ever regain these skills. If a man is injured on the left side of the head, he stands a chance of becoming mute. If a woman is hit in the same place, she'll probably keep right on talking.

Men with brain damage on the right side lost most or all of their spatial skills – the ability to think in three dimensions and to rotate objects in the mind to picture how they look from different angles. For example, an architectural plan of a house is seen two-dimensionally by a female brain, whereas a male brain can see it three-dimensionally, that is, men can see depth. Most men can see how a building would look as a finished house. Women who were brain-damaged in the exact same place on the right suffered little to no change to their spatial skills.

Doreen Kimura, Professor of Psychology at the University of Western Ontario, found that speech disorders occur in men when the left side only of the brain is damaged, but only occur in women when the frontal lobe of either hemisphere is damaged. Stuttering is a speech defect that is almost entirely restricted to males and there are three to four times as many boys as girls in remedial reading classes. Put simply, males have limited abilities when it comes to speech and conversation. This result won't surprise most women. History books show that men's lack of talk and conversation has been making women tear their hair out for thousands of years.

How the Brain is Analysed

Since the early 1990s, brain-scanning equipment has developed to the point where it is now possible to see your brain operating live on a television screen using Positron Emission Tomography (PET) scans and Magnetic Resonance Imaging (MRI). Marcus Raichle of Washington University's School of Medicine measured specific areas of increased metabolism in the brain to pinpoint the exact areas that are used for specific skills and these are shown here:

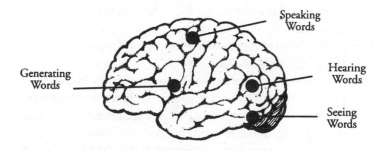

Specific hot spots in the brain using MRI

At Yale University in 1995, a team of scientists led by Drs Bennett and Shaywitz conducted tests on men and women to establish which part of the brain is used to match rhyming words. Using MRI to detect minor changes in blood flow to different parts of the brain, they confirmed that men used mainly the left brain for speech tasks while women used both left and right. These experiments and countless others carried out since the 90s all clearly show the same result: men and women's brains operate differently.

Research also shows that the left side of a girl's brain develops more rapidly than that of a boy, which means she'll speak sooner and better than her brother, read earlier, and learn a foreign language more quickly. It also explains why speech pathologists are booked solid for treatment on little boys.

Ask men and women if their brains work differently. Men will say they think they do, in fact there was something they were reading on the Internet the other day ... Women will say, of course they do – next question?

Boys, however, develop the right side of their brain faster than girls, giving them better spatial, logical and perceptual skills. Boys excel at mathematics, building, puzzles, and problem-solving, and master these much earlier than girls.

It may be fashionable to pretend that the differences between the sexes are minimal or irrelevant, but the facts simply do not support that view. Unfortunately, we now live in a social environment that insists we are the same – despite the mountain of evidence showing we are wired differently and have evolved with dramatically varying inbuilt capabilities and inclinations.

Why Women Are Better Connected

The left and right brain hemispheres are connected by a bundle of nerve fibres called the corpus callosum. This cable lets both sides of the brain communicate and exchange information.

Try to imagine you have two computers on your shoulders with an interface cable between the two. That cable is the corpus callosum.

Neurologist Roger Gorski of the University of California at Los Angeles confirmed that a woman's brain has a thicker corpus callosum than a man's, with women having up to 30% more connections between the left and right. He also proved that men and women use different parts of the brain when working on the same task. These findings have since been duplicated by other scientists elsewhere.

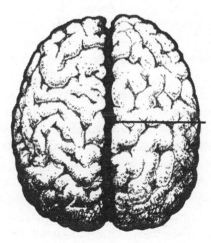

Corpus callosum

Research also reveals that the female hormone oestrogen prompts nerve cells to grow more connections within the brain and between the two hemispheres. Studies show the more connections you have, the more fluent your speech. It also explains women's ability to multi-track unrelated activities and throws a great deal of light on women's intuition. As we have discussed, a woman has a greater range of sensory equipment and, with that multiplicity of fibre connections for faster transfer of information between the hemispheres, it's no wonder a woman can make so many fast, accurate judgements about people and situations on an intuitive level.

Why Men Can Only Do One Thing at a Time!

All the available research agrees: men's brains are specialised. Compartmentalised. A male brain is configured to concentrate on one specific, dedicated task at once and most men will tell you they can only do 'one thing at a time'. When a man stops his car to read a street directory, what's the first thing he does with his radio? He turns it down! Most women can't understand why this happens. She can read while listening and talking so why can't he? Why does he insist on turning down the TV when the telephone rings? 'When he's reading the newspaper or watching TV, why can't he hear what I've just told him?' is a lament that has been made by every woman in the world at some time. The answer is that a man's brain is configured for one thing at a time because of fewer connecting fibres between the left and right hemispheres, and a more compartmentalised brain. Take a brain scan of his head when he's reading, and you'll find he is virtually deaf.

A woman's brain is configured for multi-tasking performance. She can do several unrelated things at the same time, and her brain is never disengaged, it's always active. She can talk on a telephone, at the same time as cooking a new recipe and watching television. Or she can drive a car, put on make-up and listen to the radio while talking on a hands-free telephone. But if a man is cooking a recipe and you talk to him, he is likely to become angry because he can't follow the written instructions and listen at the same time. If a man is shaving and you talk to him he'll cut himself. Most women will have had the experience of being accused by a man of making him miss a turn-off on the highway because she was chatting to him at the time. One woman told us that if she is angry with her husband, she talks to him while he is hammering a nail!

Because women use both sides of their brains, many find it more difficult to tell their left hands from their right. Around 50% of women cannot instantly recognise which is which, without looking for a ring or a freckle first. Men, on the other hand, operating in either the left or right brains, find it much easier to identify left from right. As a result, women all over the world everywhere are criticised by men for telling them to turn right – when they really meant left.

Try the Toothbrush Test

Most women can brush their teeth while walking and talking on several topics. They can make up-and-down strokes with the toothbrush at the same time as polishing a table using a circular movement with the other hand. Most men find this very difficult, if not impossible.

When men brush their teeth, their mono-tracked brain means they focus entirely on that single task. They all stand square to the basin, feet 30cm apart, body bent over the sink, moving their heads back and forth against the brush, usually to the speed of the water.

Why We Are Who We Are

At a time when we are raising boys and girls as if they are identical, science is proving they are dramatically different in their thinking. The conclusion that neurologists and brain researchers everywhere have now reached is that we are who we are because of hormones.

We are who we are because of hormones.

We are all the result of our chemistry.

Late 20th Century thinking says we are born with an empty mind and our parents, teachers and environment dictate our attitudes and choices. New research into the brain and its development now reveals that our minds are configured like a computer at around six to eight weeks after conception. Our basic 'operating system' is in place and several 'programmes' are also installed so that when we are born we come pre-packaged, like a computer with an array of add-on hardware and software.

Science also shows that the basic operating system and its wiring leave little room for change. Our environment and our teachers can only add data and run compatible programmes. And, up until now, there have been practically no 'How to' manuals available. This means that when we are born, our future choices and sexuality preferences are pre-set. Nature versus nurture? It's a done deal. Nature had the headstart from the very beginning. We now know that nurturing is a learned behaviour, with adoptive mothers proving just as effective at nurturing children as biological mothers.

Programming the Foetus

Almost all of us are made up of 46 chromosomes which are like genetic building blocks or a blueprint. Twenty-three come from our mother and 23 from our father. If our mother's 23rd chromosome is an X chromosome (it's shaped like an X) and if the father's 23rd is also an X, the result is called an XX baby, which is a girl. If the father's 23rd chromosome is a Y chromosome, we'll get an XY baby which will be a boy. The basic template for the human body and brain is female – we all start out as girls – and this is why men have female features such as nipples and mammary glands.

At the six to eight week point after conception, the foetus is more or less sexless and has the potential to develop either male or female genitalia.

German scientist Dr Gunther Dorner, a leading pioneer in social science, was one of the first to advance the theory that our sexual identity is formed six to eight weeks after conception. His research showed that if the foetus is a genetic boy (XY) it develops special cells that direct large amounts of male hormones, particularly testosterone, through the body to form male testes and configure the brain for masculine traits and behaviours, such as long-distance vision and the spatial skills for throwing, hunting and chasing.

Let's say that a male foetus (XY) needs at least one unit of male hormone to form male genitals and another three units to configure the brain with a male operating system but, for reasons we will discuss later, it does not receive the required dosage. Let's say it needs four units but receives only three. The first unit is used to form the male genitals but the brain receives only two more units which means that the brain becomes sexed two-thirds male and remains one-third female. The result is that a baby boy is born who will grow up to become a person with a mainly male brain, but with some female thinking patterns and abilities. If the male foetus only receives, say, two units of male hormone, one is used for testes formation and the brain gets only one instead of the required three. Now we have a baby whose brain is still mainly female in structure and thinking, but it is in a genetically male body. By the time puberty arrives, this boy is likely to be homosexual. We'll discuss how this happens in Chapter 8.

When the foetus is a girl (XX), little or no male hormone is present and so the body forms female genitalia and the brain's template remains female. The brain is further configured with female hormones and develops nest-defending attributes, including the centres for being able to decode verbal and non-verbal signals. When the baby girl is born, she looks female and her behaviour will be feminine as a result of her female-wired brain. But occasionally, usually by accident, the female foetus receives a significant dose of male hormone and the result is a baby girl born with, to a greater or lesser extent, a masculine brain. We will also discuss how this happens in Chapter 8.

It is estimated that about 80% to 85% of males have mainly male-wired brains and about 15% to 20% have brains that are feminised to a greater or lesser extent. Many of these in the latter group become gay.

Fifteen to twenty percent of men have feminised brains. About ten percent of women have masculinised brains.

Any references to female gender in this book will refer to approximately 90% of girls and women whose brains are wired for mainly female behaviour. Around 10% of women have a brain that is wired, to a greater or lesser extent, with some masculine abilities because it received a dose of male hormone six to eight weeks after conception.

Here is a simple but fascinating test that can show you the extent to which your brain is wired for masculine or feminine thinking. The questions have been collated from many leading studies into human brain sexuality and the rating system used was developed by British geneticist Anne Moir. There are no right or wrong answers in this test, but it gives you some interesting insights into why you make the choices you make and think the way you do. At the end of the test you can score your result on the chart. Photocopy the test and give it to those you live and work with, and the result will be a real eye-opener for everyone.

The Brain-Wiring Test

This test is designed to indicate the masculinity or femininity of your brain patterns. There are no right or wrong answers – the result is simply an indication of the probable level of male hormone your brain did, or did not, receive around six to eight weeks after your conception. This is reflected in your preference of values, behaviours, style, orientations and choices.

Circle the statement that is most likely to be true for you most of the time.

1. When it comes to reading a map or street directory you:
    a. have difficulty and often ask for help
    b. turn it round to face the direction you're going

    c. have no difficulty reading maps or street
       directories

2. **You're cooking a complicated meal with the radio
   playing and a friend phones. Do you:**
    a. leave the radio on and continue cooking while
       talking on the phone
    b. turn the radio off, talk and keep cooking
    c. say you'll call them back as soon as you've
       finished cooking

3. **Friends are coming to visit and ask for directions
   to your new house. Do you:**
    a. draw a map with clear directions and send it
       to them or get someone else to explain how to
       get there
    b. ask what landmarks they know then try to
       explain to them how to get there
    c. explain verbally how to get there: 'Take the
       M3 to Newcastle, turn off, turn left, go to the
       second traffic lights ...'

4. **When explaining an idea or concept, are you
   more likely to:**
    a. use a pencil, paper and body language gestures
    b. explain it verbally using body language and
       gestures
    c. explain it verbally, being clear and concise

5. **When coming home from a great movie, you
   prefer to:**
    a. picture scenes from the movie in your mind
    b. talk about the scenes and what was said

c. quote mainly what was said in the movie

6. **In a cinema, you usually prefer to sit:**
    a. on the right side
    b. anywhere
    c. on the left side

7. **A friend has something mechanical that won't work. You would:**
    a. sympathise, and discuss how they feel about it
    b. recommend someone reliable who can fix it
    c. figure out how it works and attempt to fix it for them

8. **You're in an unfamiliar place and someone asks you where North is. You:**
    a. confess you don't know
    b. guess where it is, after a bit of thought
    c. point towards North without difficulty

9. **You've found a parking space but it's tight and you must reverse into it. You would:**
    a. rather try to find another space
    b. carefully attempt to back into it
    c. reverse into it without any difficulty.

10. **You are watching TV when the telephone rings. You would:**
    a. answer the phone with the TV on
    b. turn the TV down and then answer
    c. turn the TV off, tell others to be quiet and then answer

11. **You've just heard a new song by your favourite artist. Usually you:**
    a. can sing some of the song afterwards without difficulty
    b. can sing some of it afterwards if it's a really simple song
    c. find it hard to remember how the song sounded but you might recall some of the words

12. **You are best at predicting outcomes by:**
    a. using intuition
    b. making a decision based on both the available information and 'gut feeling'
    c. using facts, statistics and data

13. **You've misplaced your keys. Would you:**
    a. do something else until the answer comes to you
    b. do something else, but keep trying to remember where you put them
    c. mentally retrace your steps until you remember where you left them

14. **You're in a hotel room and you hear the distant sound of a siren. You:**
    a. couldn't identify where it's coming from
    b. could probably point to it if you concentrate
    c. could point straight to where it's coming from

15. **You go to a social meeting and are introduced to seven or eight new people. Next day you:**
    a. can easily picture their faces
    b. would remember a few of their faces
    c. would be more likely to remember their names

16. **You want to go to the country for your holiday but your partner wants to go to a beach resort. To convince them your idea is better, you:**
    a. tell them sweetly how you feel: you love the countryside and the kids and family always have fun there
    b. tell them if they go to the country you'll be grateful and will be happy to go to the beach next time
    c. use the facts: the country resort is closer, cheaper, and well-organised for sporting and leisure activities

17. **When planning your day's activities, you usually:**
    a. write a list so you can see what needs to be done
    b. think of the things you need to do
    c. picture in your mind the people you will see, places you will visit and things you'll be doing

18. **A friend has a personal problem and has come to discuss it with you. You:**
    a. are sympathetic and understanding
    b. say that problems are never as bad as they seem and explain why
    c. give suggestions or rational advice on how to solve the problem

19. **Two friends from different marriages are having a secret affair. How likely are you to spot it?**
    a. you could spot it very early
    b. you'd pick up on it half the time
    c. you'd probably miss it

20. **What is life all about, as you see it?**
    a. having friends and living in harmony with those around you
    b. being friendly to others while maintaining personal independence
    c. achieving worthwhile goals, earning others' respect and winning prestige and advancement

21. **Given the choice, you would prefer to work:**
    a. in a team where people are compatible
    b. around others but maintaining your own space
    c. by yourself

22. **The books you prefer to read are:**
    a. novels and fiction
    b. magazines and newspapers
    c. non-fiction, autobiographies

23. **When you go shopping you tend to:**
    a. often buy on impulse, particularly the specials
    b. have a general plan but take it as it comes
    c. read the labels and compare costs

24. **You prefer to go to bed, wake up and eat meals:**
    a. whenever you feel like it
    b. on a basic schedule but you are flexible
    c. at about the same time each day

25. **You've started a new job and met lots of new people on the staff. One of them phones you when you are at home. You would:**
    a. find it easy to recognise their voice
    b. recognise it about half the time

c. have difficulty identifying the voice

26. **What upsets you most when arguing with someone?**
    a. their silence or lack of response
    b. when they won't see your point of view
    c. their probing or challenging questions and comments

27. **In school how did you feel about spelling tests and writing essays?**
    a. you found them both fairly easy
    b. you were generally OK with one but not the other
    c. you weren't very good at either

28. **When it comes to dancing or jazz routines, you:**
    a. can 'feel' the music once you've learnt the steps
    b. can do some exercises or dances, but get lost with others
    c. have difficulty keeping time or rhythm

29. **How good are you at identifying and mimicking animal sounds?**
    a. not very good
    b. reasonable
    c. very good

30. **At the end of a long day, you usually prefer to:**
    a. talk to friends or family about your day
    b. listen to others talk about their day
    c. read a paper, watch TV and not talk

How to Score the Test

First, add the number of A, B and C responses and use the following table to arrive at your final result.

For Males

Number of A's x 10 points =

Number of B's   x 5 points =

Number of C's x -5 points =

               Total points =

For Females

Number of A's x 15 points =

Number of B's   x 5 points =

Number of C's x -5 points =

               Total points =

For any questions where the answers didn't accurately reflect your life or you left them blank, award yourself five points.

Analysing the Result

Most males will score between 0–180 and most females, 150–300. Brains that are 'wired' for mainly masculine thinking usually score below 150. The closer to 0 they are, the more masculine they are, and the higher their testosterone level is likely to be. These people demonstrate strong logical, analytical and verbal skills and tend to be disciplined and well-organised. The closer to 0 they score, the better they are at projecting costs and planning outcomes for statistical data, with their emotions hardly influencing

The Brain-Wiring Test

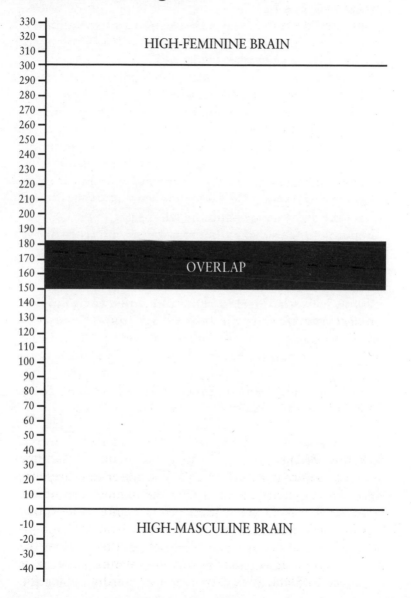

them at all. Scores in the minus range are high masculine scores. These scores show that large amounts of testosterone were present in the early stages of the foetal development. The lower the score for a woman, the more likely she will be to have lesbian tendencies.

Brains that are wired for mainly feminine thinking will score higher than 180. The higher the number, the more feminine the brain will be, and the more likely the person is to demonstrate significant creative, artistic and musical talents. They will make more of their decisions on intuition or gut feeling, and are good at recognising problems using minimal data. They are also good at solving problems using creativity and insight. The higher the score is above 180 for a man, the greater the chance he will be gay.

Males who score below 0 and women who score above 300 have brains that are wired so oppositely that the only thing they are likely to have in common is that they live on the same planet!

Scores between 150–180 show compatibility of thought for both sexes, or a foot in both sexual camps. These people do not show a bias for either male or female thinking and usually demonstrate a flexibility in thinking that can be a significant advantage to any group who are going through a problem-solving process. They have the predisposition to make friends with both men and women.

A Final Word

Since the beginning of the 1980s, our knowledge of the brain has surpassed our wildest expectations. US President George Bush proclaimed the 1990s as the Decade of the Brain and we have now entered the Millennium of the Mind. In our discussion of the brain and its various regions we have simplified neuroscience to avoid being too technical, but we are also conscious of not over-simplifying because the brain is a web-like structure of neurons that form complex assemblies of brain cells which make up brain regions.

You, the reader, don't want to become a neuroscientist, you just want a basic understanding of brain function and some strategies that work when dealing with the opposite sex. It's easy to pinpoint the area of the brain used for spatial skill in males and to develop working strategies for it. It's much more difficult to get a handle on the exact operation of emotion in the brain. But, even so, we can still develop workable strategies for dealing with it.

CHAPTER 4
TALKING AND LISTENING

What females say

What males hear

Barbara and Allan were getting ready to go to a cocktail party. Barbara had bought a new dress and was anxious to look her best. She held up two pairs of shoes, one blue, one gold. Then she asked Allan the question that all men fear, 'Darling, which should I wear with this dress?'

A cold chill ran down Allan's back. He knew he was in trouble. 'Ahh ... umm ... whichever you like sweetheart,' he stammered. 'Come on Allan,' she said, impatiently. 'Which looks better ... blue or gold?' 'Gold!' he replied, nervously. 'So, what's wrong with the blue?' she asked. 'You've never liked them! I paid a fortune for them and you hate them, don't you?'

Allan's shoulders slumped. 'If you don't want my opinion, Barbara, don't ask!' he said. He thought he'd been asked to fix a problem but, when he solved it, she wasn't at all grateful. Barbara, however, was using a typical female speech trait: indirect speech. She'd already decided which shoes she was going to wear and didn't want another opinion on it; she wanted confirmation that she looked good. In this chapter, we will look at the problems men and women have communicating with each other and offer some novel solutions.

The 'Blue or Gold Shoes' Strategy

If a woman asks 'blue or gold?' when selecting shoes, it's important that a man does not give an answer. Instead, he should ask, 'Have you chosen a pair, darling?' Most women are taken aback by this approach because most men they know immediately state a preference. 'Well ... I thought I could possibly wear the gold ...' she'll say, uncertainly. The reality is, she has already chosen the gold shoes. 'Why the gold?' he'll ask. 'Because I'm wearing gold accessories and my dress has a gold pattern in it,' she'll respond. A skilled man would then reply, 'Wow! Great choice! You'll look fabulous! You've done well! I love it!' And you can bet he'll have a great night.

Why Males Can't Talk Proper

We've known for thousands of years that men aren't great conversationalists, particularly when compared to women. Not only do girls start speaking earlier than boys but a three-year-old girl has nearly twice the vocabulary of a three-year-old boy, with her speech almost 100% comprehensible. Speech pathologists are kept busy with parents bringing young boys in for therapy with the same complaint: 'He can't speak properly.' If the boy has an older sister, this speech difference is even more noticeable, particularly as older sisters and mothers frequently talk for their sons. Ask a five-year-old boy, 'How are you?' and his mother or sister answers, 'He's fine, thanks'.

Mothers, daughters, and older sisters often speak on behalf of the males in their family.

For males, speech and language are not critical brain skills. They operate mainly in the left brain and have no specific location. Studies with left brain-damaged people show that most speech disorders in males occur in the left/rear hemisphere and mainly in the left/front for females. When a male talks, MRI scans show that his entire left hemisphere becomes active as it searches to find a centre for speaking, but is unable to find much. Consequently, men aren't much good at talking.

The following MRI brain scan is from research conducted by Dr Tonmoy Sharma, head of cognitive psychopharmacology at the Institute of Psychiatry, London, in 1999. As you can see, males have few hot spots for speech functions.

This demonstrates why boys tend to mumble and have sloppier pronunciation than girls. They use fillers like 'um', 'uh' and 'like' during conversation, are more likely to drop the 'g' from the end of words, saying comin' and goin', and using only three tones of voice when speaking, compared to a woman's five tones. When men get together to watch a football match on TV, that's exactly what they do – the only conversation tends to be 'pass the chips' and 'got any more beer?' For a group of women, meeting up to watch a TV programme has always been more of an excuse for a chat. As a result, they'll tend to get together to watch something like a TV soap, where the characters and the plots are familiar, rather than a complicated murder-mystery drama.

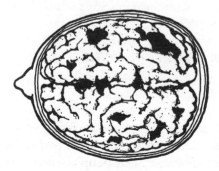

Location of male speech and language. (Black areas represent activity.) Institute of Psychiatry, London, 1999.

The different ways the sexes express themselves is perhaps nowhere more obvious than in sport. Watch any TV sporting event and observe how female basketball players, for instance, can describe their match exactly, succintly and perfectly comprehensibly. When male players are interviewed, however, not only is it difficult to make sense of the little they have to say, but their mouths don't appear to move. With teenagers, the difference is remarkable, too. When we asked our teenage daughter about the party she attended the night before, she gave an articulate recitation of everything that happened – who said what to whom, how everyone felt about it and what they were wearing. Our teenage son, asked the same question, mumbled, 'Uhh ... good.'

On Valentine's Day, florists tell men to 'say it with flowers' because they know that a man finds it difficult to say it with words. Buying a card is never a problem for a man, it's what to write inside that stumps him.

Men often choose greetings cards

with plenty of words inside. That

way, there's less space for them to write.

Men evolved as lunch-chasers remember, not communicators. The hunt was conducted with a series of non-verbal signals and often the hunters would sit for hours silently watching for their prey. They didn't talk or bond. When modern men go fishing together, they can sit for hours and say nothing. They're having a great time enjoying each other's company, but they don't feel the need to express it in words. Yet if women were spending time together and not talking, it would be indicative of a major problem. The only time men come close is when the division of communication in the tightly compartmentalised male brain is broken down – by copious quantities of alcohol.

Boys and their Schooling

In the beginning, boys don't do well at school because their verbal abilities are inferior to those of girls. As a result, they perform poorly in languages, English and the arts. They feel stupid in front of the more articulate girls and become boisterous and disruptive. The idea of starting boys at school a year later, when their language development would be on a par with girls a year younger, would, in that respect, seem to make a lot of sense. It would leave boys feeling a great deal better about themselves, and much less intimidated by the fluency of girls the same age.

In later years, girls fall behind in physics and sciences where spatial ability is vital. But while remedial language classes are full of boys whose worried parents hope and pray that their sons will eventually be able to read, write and speak properly, no such caveat is put on girls to brush up on their spatial reasoning. They simply end up changing subjects.

There has been a growing trend in recent years to separate boys and girls in certain subjects like English, maths and sciences. Shenfield High School in Essex, for example, allows each sex to learn in an environment where there is no competition from the opposite sex. In maths tests, the girls are asked questions that relate to a garden setting, whereas the boys' tests are set in a hardware store. This type of segregation capitalises on the natural preferences of male and female brain-wiring and the results are impressive. In English, the boys' results are four times higher than the national average and the girls' maths and science scores are almost double those in other schools.

Why Women Are Great Talkers

With women, speech is a specific area located primarily in the front left hemisphere with another, smaller specific area in the right hemisphere. Having speech on both sides of the brain makes women good conversationalists. They enjoy it, and do lots of it. With specific areas to control speech, the rest of a woman's brain is available for other tasks, enabling her to do lots of different things at once while talking.

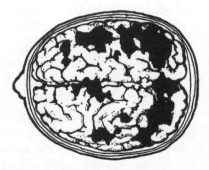

Location of female speech and language. (Black areas represent activity.) Institute of Psychiatry, London, 1999.

Compare the above illustration, which shows the locations of speech and language in women, to that of men, and you can see why women are such excellent communicators and men are not.

Recent research has shown that a baby learns to recognise its mother's voice while it is still in the womb, probably from voice resonance through the mother's body. A four-day-old baby can distinguish the speech patterns of its native tongue from a foreign language. At four months, babies can recognise lip movements associated with vowel sounds. Before their first birthday, they are beginning to associate words with meanings; by eighteen months, they have the beginnings of a vocabulary that, at two years old, will have expanded in the case of girls to up to 2,000 words. Both intellectually and physically, this is an awesome achievement compared to the learning abilities of an adult.

Having a specific brain zone for speech allows girls to learn foreign languages faster and easier than boys, and it also explains why girls are better at grammar, punctuation and spelling. In 25 years of giving seminars in foreign countries, we have rarely been given a male translator – they're usually women.

Subject	Number of Teachers	% Women	% Men
Spanish	2,700	78	22
French	16,200	75	25
German	8,100	75	25
Drama	8,900	67	33
Other languages	1,300	70	30

This chart shows how women clearly dominate subjects where strong left-brain verbal ability is required. Women's specific speech centres give them superiority in language ability and verbal dexterity.

These figures show that even in the most politically correct areas – education and government – male and female brain-orientation strongly influences a teacher's subject choices. Equal Opportunity groups feel that they are doing a good job because half of all teachers are men and half are women but, as you can see, females clearly dominate the areas involving speech.

The left brain controls the physical functions of the right side of the body, which could be why most people write with the right hand. This would also explain why the handwriting of most women is much more legible than that of men – women's specific language centres are pre-wired for better use of language, both spoken and written.

Why Women Need to Talk

Male brains are highly compartmentalised and have the ability to separate and store information. At the end of a day full of problems, a man's mono-tracking brain can file them all away. The female brain does not store information in this way – the problems just keep going around and around in her head.

Men can mentally index their problems

and put them on hold. Women churn.

The only way a woman gets rid of her problems from her mind is by talking about them to acknowledge them. Therefore, when a woman talks at the end of the day, her objective is to discharge the problems, not to find conclusions or solutions.

The Hormonal Connection

Scientist Elizabeth Hanson of the University of Western Ontario conducted a study on women's performance and the hormone oestrogen. Hanson found that low testosterone levels depressed a woman's spatial ability, while high oestrogen enhanced her articulation and fine-motor skills. This explains why, during the menstrual cycle, on high oestrogen days a woman can behave calmly and speak with near-perfect articulation. Conversely, on high testosterone days her speech is more erratic but her spatial ability is better – she might not be so expert at humiliating a man with a well-placed barb, but she could hit him with a frying pan from a distance of 10 metres.

Women Love to Talk

When women sit together to watch a movie on TV, they usually talk simultaneously about a variety of subjects, including children, men, careers and what's happening in their lives. When groups of men and women watch a movie together, the men usually end up telling the women to shut up. Men can either talk *or* watch the screen – they can't do both – and they don't understand that women can. Besides, women consider that the point of all getting together is to have a good time and develop relationships – not just to sit there like couch potatoes staring at the screen.

During the ad breaks, a man often asks a woman to explain the storyline and tell him where the relationship between the characters is going. He is unable, unlike women, to read the subtle body language signals that reveal how the characters are feeling emotionally. Since women originally spent their days with the other women and children in the group, they developed the ability to communicate successfully in order to maintain relationships. For a woman, speech continues to have such a clear purpose: to build relationships and make friends. For men, to talk is to relate the facts.

Men see the telephone as a communication tool for relaying facts and information to other people, but a woman sees it as a means of bonding. A woman can spend two weeks on vacation with her girlfriend and, when she returns home, telephone the same girlfriend and talk for another two hours.

There is no convincing evidence that social conditioning, the fact that girls' mothers talked to them more, is the reason why girls talk more than boys. Psychiatrist Dr Michael Lewis, author of *Social Behaviour and Language Acquisition*, conducted experiments that found mothers talked to, and looked at, baby girls more often than baby boys. Scientific evidence shows parents respond to the brain bias of their children. Since a girl's brain is better organised to send and receive speech, we therefore talk to them more. Consequently, mothers who try to talk to their sons are usually disappointed to receive only short grunts in reply.

Men Talk Silently to Themselves

Men evolved as warriors, protectors and problem solvers. Their brain bias and social conditioning prevent them from showing fear or uncertainty. This is why, when a man is asked to solve a problem, he will often say, 'Can you leave it with me?' or 'I'll think it over.' And that is exactly what he does – he thinks it over silently, with an expressionless face. Only when he has the answer will he speak or look animated to show he is ready to communicate the solution. Men talk mainly inside their heads because they don't have the verbal capability that women have to use words externally for communication. When a man is sitting staring out of a window, a brain scan shows that he is having a conversation with himself – inside his head. When a woman sees a man doing this, she assumes that he's bored or idle, and tries to talk to him or give him something to do. A man will often become angry when interrupted. As we know, he can't do more than one thing at once.

The Downside of Silent Talk

If a man is dealing with other men, talking inside his head is not a problem. Men can sit with each other in a meeting for long periods of time with little speech and no-one feels uneasy about it – it's just like fishing. Men often enjoy a 'quiet drink' after work and that's exactly what it is – quiet.

If a man is with a woman or a group of women, the women are likely to think he is distant, sulky or simply doesn't want to join in. If men want to get on better with women, then they need to talk more.

Women Think Aloud

'My wife drives me crazy when she's got a problem or is talking about what she intends to do that day,' said a man at one of our seminars. 'She talks out loud about the options, possibilities, people involved, what she needs to do and where she'll be going. It's so distracting, I can't concentrate on anything!'

A woman will verbalise a series of items out loud in random order, listing all the options and possibilities.

A woman's brain is pre-wired to use speech as a main form of expression and this is one of her strengths. If a man has to carry out a list of five or six tasks, he will say, 'I've got some things to do. I'll see you later'. A woman will verbalise all the items out loud in random order, mentioning all options and possibilities. She will say, 'Let's see, I've got to pick up the dry cleaning and get the car washed – by the way, Ray rang and wants you to call him back – then I'll pick up the parcel from the Post Office, I suppose I could also ...' This is one of the reasons men accuse women of talking too much.

The Downside of Thinking Aloud

Women perceive thinking aloud as being friendly and sharing, but men see it differently. On a personal level, a man thinks the woman is giving him a list of problems that she expects him to fix, so he becomes anxious, upset or tries to tell her what to do. In a business meeting, men view a woman thinking aloud as being scatterbrained, undisciplined or unintelligent. To impress men in business, a woman needs to keep her thoughts inside her head and only talk about conclusions. In a relationship, partners need to discuss their different ways of working through problems. Men need to understand that when a woman talks, she is not expecting him to respond with solutions. Women need to understand that when a man doesn't talk, that is not a cue that something is wrong.

Women Talk, Men Feel Nagged

The building of relationships through talk is a priority in the brain-wiring of women. Italian women are the top talkers speaking up to 6,000–8,000 words a day. They use an additional 2,000–3,000 vocal sounds to communicate, as well as 8,000–10,000 gestures, facial expressions, head movements and other body signals. This gives these women a daily average of more than 20,000 communication 'words' to relate their messages. Western women speak up to 80% of that figure. That explains just why the British Medical Association recently reported that women are four times more likely to suffer with jaw problems.

'Once I didn't talk to my wife for six months', said the comedian. 'I didn't want to interrupt'.

Contrast a woman's daily 'chatter' to that of a man. He utters just 2,000–4,000 words and 1,000–2,000 vocal sounds, and makes a mere 2,000–3,000 body language signals. His daily average adds up to around 7,000 communication 'words' – just over a third the output of most women.

This speech difference becomes apparent at the end of the day when a man and a woman sit down together for dinner. He's completed his 7,000 'words' and has no desire to communicate any more. Her state depends on what she has been doing that day. If she's spent the day talking with people, she may have used her quota of 'words' and also has little desire to say much more. If she's been home with young children she will be lucky to have used 2–3,000 'words'. She still has up to 15,000 to go! We're all familiar with friction at the dinner table.

> *Fiona:* 'Hi Darling ... it's good to see you back home. How was your day?'
>
> *Mike:* 'Good.'
>
> *Fiona:* 'Brian told me that you were going to finalise that big deal with Peter Thomson today. How did it go?'
>
> *Mike:* 'Fine.'
>
> *Fiona:* 'That's good. He can be a really tough customer. Do you think he'll take your advice?'
>
> *Mike:* 'Yeah.'
>
> *... and so on.*

Mike feels as though he's being interrogated and becomes annoyed. He just wants 'peace and quiet'. Attempting to avoid an argument about why he won't talk, he asks: 'How was your day?'

And so she tells him. And tells him. Every detail of what happened in her day.

'Well ... what a day I had! I decided not to go to the city today because my cousin's best friend works at the bus station and he said there'd be a strike today so I decided to walk. The weather forecaster said it would be a sunny day so I decided to wear my blue dress – you know the one – I bought it in America – anyway ... as I was walking I bumped into Susan and ...'

She begins speaking the balance of her unspoken words. He wonders why she won't shut up and leave him in peace. He feels like he's been 'nagged to death'! 'All I want is a bit of peace and quiet!' is the cry of men everywhere. He's a hunter. He's been chasing lunch all day. He just wants to stare into the fire. The problem comes, however, when she starts feeling ignored and becomes resentful.

When a man is silent, it's easy for a woman to start feeling unloved.

The point of the woman's talk is to talk. But the man sees her continual talk about problems as a plea for solutions. With his analytical brain, he continually interrupts her.

> *Fiona:* '... and I slipped on the pavement and broke the heel on my new shoes, and then ...'
>
> *Mike:* (Interrupting) 'Wait a minute Fiona ... you shouldn't wear high heels to the shopping centre! I've seen a survey on it. It's dangerous – wear trainers – it's safer!'

He thinks, Problem solved!

She thinks, Why doesn't he keep quiet and
just listen? She continues –

Fiona: '... and when I got back to the car, the back
tyre was flat and so ...'

Mike: (Interrupting) 'Look, what you should do is
get the tyre pressure checked when you fill
up at the garage. That way you won't be
stuck like that again!'

He thinks, That's another problem I've solved for her.

She thinks, Why doesn't he keep quiet and listen?

He thinks, Why won't she keep quiet now and leave me
alone? Do I have to solve all her problems for
her? Why can't she get it right the first time?

She ignores his interruptions and keeps talking.

We have surveyed thousands of women everywhere and
they all make one point clear:

When a woman is speaking her

unused words at the end of the day,

she doesn't want interruptions

with solutions to her problems.

This is good news for men – you're not expected to respond,
just to listen. When a woman has finished speaking she feels
relieved and happy. Plus she'll think you're a wonderful man
for listening, so you'll probably have a good night.

Talking about day-to-day problems is how modern women
cope with stress. They see it as bonding and being supportive.
This is why most people who go to counsellors are women,
and most counsellors are women who are trained to listen.

Why Couples Fail

Seventy-four per cent of working women and 98% of non-working women name the biggest failing of their husbands and boyfriends as a reluctance to talk, particularly at the end of the day. Past generations of women never felt this problem because they always had lots of children and other women for conversation and support. Now mothers who stay at home are likely to feel isolated and lonely because their female neighbours are all likely to be at work. Working women have less difficulty with non-talking males because they have been speaking to others during the day. None of this is anyone's fault. We are the first generation to have no suitable role models for successful relationships. Our parents never had these problems. But the good news is that we can learn the new skills required for survival.

How Men Talk

A man's sentences are shorter than a woman's and are more structured. They usually have a simple opening, a clear point and a conclusion. It's easy to follow what he means or wants. If you multi-track several subjects with a man, he gets lost. It's important for a woman to understand that if you want to be convincing or persuasive with a man, you should present only one clear thought or idea at a time.

The first rule of talking to a man:

Keep it simple! Give him only

one thing at a time to think about.

If you are presenting an idea to a mixed group of men and women, it's safer to use a male speaking structure to make your points. Both sexes can follow 'man-talk' but men have difficulty following a woman's multi-tracked conversations and can quickly lose interest.

Women Multi-Track

With a greater flow of information between left and right hemispheres and specific brain locations for speech, most women can talk about several subjects simultaneously – sometimes in a single sentence. It's like juggling three or four balls at the one time and most women seem to do it effortlessly. Not only that, but women can juggle several subjects with other women who are all doing the same thing – and no-one ever seems to drop a ball.

At the end of the conversation, each woman knows something about the several subjects being discussed, the events that took place and the meaning of each. This multi-tracking ability is frustrating for a man as the male brain is mono-tracked and can only handle one subject at a time. When a group of women are multi-tracking several subjects, men can become completely dazed and confused.

A woman may start talking about one subject, switch in mid-sentence to another and then, without any warning, revert back to the first with a little bit of something completely different dropped in for good measure. Men become perplexed and befuddled. Take this family conversation from the Pease household:

> *Allan:* 'Now, wait a minute – who said what to whom at the office?'
> *Barbara:* 'I wasn't talking about the office – I was talking about my brother-in-law.'

> *Allan:* 'Your brother-in-law? You didn't tell me
> you'd changed the subject!'
> *Barbara:* 'Well, you'll just have to pay closer attention.
> Everyone else understands.'
> *Fiona:* 'Yes – I knew what she meant. It's perfectly
> (Sister) clear to me.'
>
> *Jasmine:* 'So did I. Dad, you're so dumb! You never
> (Daughter) follow anything!'
> *Allan:* 'Oh, I give up with you women!'
> *Cameron:* 'Yeah, me too, and I'm only a kid!'
> (Son)

Men may be able to find their way from

A to B via a maze of back streets, but put

them in the middle of a group of women

discussing a number of topics at the

same time, and they get completely lost.

This kind of facility for complex multi-tracking is common to nearly all women. Just take secretaries. For their jobs, performing a number of different tasks at once is an absolute necessity. It's hardly surprising then that of the 716,148 secretaries in the UK in 1998, 99.1% were women – there were only 5,913 men. Some groups attribute this to girls being groomed for such careers while still at school. That fails to take into account, however, women's domination of verbal, organisational and multi-tracking abilities. Even in fields where hierarchies are strongly committed to Equal Opportunity policies, such as community work, counselling and in the welfare system, of the 144,266 people employed to do these jobs in Britain in 1998, 43,816 were men and 100,450 were women. Wherever communication skills and verbal prowess is required, women reign supreme.

What Brain Scans Show

When a woman is speaking, brain scans show that her front left and right brain centres controlling speech are both operating. Her hearing functions also operate at the same time. This powerful multi-tracking capability allows a woman to speak and listen simultaneously and to do both on several unrelated topics. Men are awestruck when they first learn that women have this ability – they just thought that women were a noisy lot.

Women can speak and listen simultaneously, while at the same time accusing men of being able to do neither.

Women have been the butt of jokes from men for thousands of years on the issue of how much they talk. At conferences in every country we hear men say the same things: 'Listen to those women all talking – blah, blah, blah – no-one listening!' Chinese, German and Norwegians say it just as much as African and Inuit men. But the difference is, when men say it, they take it in turns. For, as we now know, men can either speak or listen – they can't do both at once.

Strategies for Talking with Men

Men usually only interrupt each other if they are becoming competitive or aggressive. If you want to communicate with a man, a simple strategy is not to interrupt when he is speaking. This is difficult for a woman because for her, simultaneous talk builds relationships and shows participation. She has an urge to multi-track the conversation to impress him or make him feel significant. When she does it, however, he effectively becomes deaf. He will also resent what he considers a rude interruption.

Men take turns talking, so when a

man is having his turn, let him have it.

'Stop interrupting me!' is shouted by men at women everywhere and in every language. A man's sentences are solution-oriented and he needs to get to the end of the sentence, otherwise the conversation seems pointless. He can't multi-track various points at different times in the conversation and he views anyone else doing it as impolite or scatter-brained. This is a foreign concept to a woman. She multi-tracks to build rapport and make him feel important. To add insult to injury, in a typical male/female conversation, 76% of interruptions are made by men!

Why Men Love Big Words

Having no specific brain location for speech, the hunter needed to be able to communicate the most amount of information with the least number of words, so his brain developed specific areas for vocabulary, located in the front and rear part of the left brain. In women, vocabulary is front and back of both hemispheres and is not a strong ability. Consequently, definition and the meaning of words is not important to a woman because she relies on voice intonation for meaning and body language for emotional content.

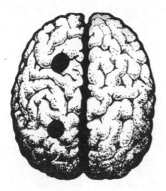

Location of vocabulary in the male brain

This is why the meaning of words is so important to men and why they will use definition to gain advantage over another man or woman. Men use language to compete with one another and definition becomes an important tactic in playing the game. If one man is trying to make a strong or forceful point and says, for example, '... he wasn't making his point clearly or getting to the bottom line so that everyone could understand what he meant', another man may interrupt with, 'He didn't articulate?', to better define the point being made and 'get one up' on the first man. Or the competitive man may use the word *'articulate'* to summarise the other person's entire sentence.

Women Use Words for Reward

A woman uses words to show participation and build relationships and so, for her, words are a form of reward. If she likes you, is agreeing with what you are saying or wants to be your friend, she'll talk to you a lot. The reverse is also true. If she wants to punish you or let you know she's not your friend, she won't talk. Men often call this 'the silent treatment' and the threat from a woman of 'I'll never talk to you again!' is one to be taken seriously.

> *If a woman is talking to you a lot,*
>
> *she likes you. If she's not talking*
>
> *to you, you're in trouble.*

It takes an average man around nine minutes of silence to realise that he's being punished. Until the nine minutes' mark is reached, he sees her silence as a kind of bonus – he's getting some 'peace and quiet'. Men everywhere complain that women talk too much. Certainly, compared to men, they talk a great deal.

Women Are Indirect

It started out as a nice, relaxing weekend drive through a beautiful valley a few hours away from home. As the road twisted and turned around the mountainside, John switched the radio off to better concentrate on the road. He couldn't navigate bends and listen to music at the same time.

'John,' said his girlfriend Allison, 'would you like a cup of coffee?'

John smiled. 'No thanks, I'm fine,' he replied, thinking to himself how nice it was of her to ask. A short time later John noticed that Allison had stopped talking, and suspected he might have done something wrong. 'Everything OK darling?' he enquired. 'Just fine!' she snapped. Confused, he asked, 'So ... what's the problem?' She snorted with derision. 'You wouldn't stop!' she said. John's analytical mind tried to remember when she had used the word *'stop'*. He was sure she hadn't and told her so. She told him he needed to be more sensitive. When she had asked him if he wanted coffee, what she really meant was that she wanted one. 'Am I supposed to be a mind reader?' he asked sarcastically.

'Get to the point please!' is another command barked by men to women everywhere. When a woman talks she uses indirect speech which means that she hints at what she wants or beats around the bush. Indirect speech is a female speciality and serves a specific purpose – it builds relationships and rapport with others by avoiding aggression, confrontation or discord. It fits perfectly into the nest-defender's overall approach to preserving harmony.

Indirect talk builds rapport among women

– but it often doesn't work with men

because they don't understand the rules.

Women's brains are process-oriented and they enjoy the process of communicating. Men find this lack of structure and purpose very disconcerting, and accuse women of not knowing what they're talking about. In business, indirect speech can be disastrous for women as men can't follow a multi-tracked indirect conversation, and may end up turning down their proposals, requests or bids for advancement. Indirect speech may be excellent for building relationships but, unfortunately, that benefit may pale into insignificance if cars or planes end up crashing when the driver or pilot is unclear about what is being said.

Indirect speech usually includes a lot of qualifiers such as 'kind of', 'sort of' and 'a bit'. Imagine if Winston Churchill had used indirect speech to try to motivate the Allies against the threat from Hitler. It wouldn't have sounded quite the same.

'We will fight them on the beaches – kind of – we will fight them a bit in the fields – we will never, sort of, surrender.' They might even have ended up losing the war.

When a woman uses indirect speech with another woman there is never a problem – women are sensitive to picking up the real meaning. It can, however, be disastrous using it with men. Men use direct speech and take words literally. But with patience and practice, men and women can learn to understand one another.

Men Are Direct

Men's sentences are short, direct, solution-oriented and to the point, drawing on a broader vocabulary and peppered with facts. They use quantifiers such as *'none'*, *'never'* and *'absolutely'*. This kind of speech helps close business deals quickly and efficiently, and is a means of asserting authority over others. When men use such direct speech in their social relationships, it often makes them appear abrupt and rude.

Consider these statements:
Go and make an omelette for breakfast!
Make me an omelette for breakfast, will you?
Would you make me an omelette for breakfast please?
Do you think we should have an omelette for breakfast?
Wouldn't it be great to have an omelette for breakfast?
Do you feel like an omelette for breakfast?

These requests for an omelette go from completely direct to completely indirect. The first three statements are most likely to be used by men, and the last three by women. All have the same request expressed in a different way. It is easy, sometimes, to see how an appetite for an omelette can all end in tears, with her saying, 'You ignorant pig! Make it yourself!' and him saying, 'You're not capable of making a decision. I'm going to McDonald's!'

What to Do About It

Men need to understand that indirect talk is part of a woman's wiring and they should not get upset about it. To build a personal relationship with a woman, a man needs to listen effectively, using 'listening sounds' and body language (we'll come to that in a moment). He doesn't need to volunteer solutions or question her motives. If a woman sounds like she may have a problem, an excellent technique for a man to use is to ask her, 'Do you want me to listen as a boy or a girl?' If she wants him to be a girl, he just listens and encourages her. If she says she wants him to be a boy, he can offer solutions.

To get a man to listen, give him advance

notice and provide an agenda.

In order to make the most impact on a man, tell him what you want to talk about and when. For example: 'I'd like to talk with you about how to handle a problem I have with my boss at work. Would after dinner at seven o'clock be a good time for you to talk me through it?' This appeals to the logical structure of man's brain, makes him feel appreciated and passes on the problem! An indirect approach would be, 'No-one appreciates me', which creates problems because a man is likely to think that he's being blamed and goes straight on the defensive. Direct speech is the way men do business with other men in Western countries but this is not the case in the East. In Japan, for example, indirect speech is widely used as a business language and people who use direct language are considered childish or naïve. Foreigners who use it are seen as immature.

How to Motivate a Man to Action

Having a Masters Degree in indirect talk, a woman asks 'can' and 'could' questions: 'Can you take the rubbish out?' 'Could you call me tonight?' 'Can you pick up the kids?' A man interprets her words literally so when she asks, 'Can you change the lightbulb?' he hears, 'Do you have the ability to change the lightbulb?' A man interprets questions beginning with 'can' or 'could' as a check of his ability so his logical response is Yes, he *can* take rubbish out or he *could* change the lightbulb, but these words carry no commitment to act. Plus, men feel manipulated and forced into giving a 'yes' response.

To motivate a man, ask 'will' or 'would' questions to get commitment. For example, 'Will you call me tonight?' asks for a commitment to tonight and a man must answer 'Yes' or 'No'. You are better off getting a 'No' answer to a 'will you' or 'would you' question and know where you stand than get a 'Yes' to every 'can you' or 'could you' question you ask. A man who asks a woman to marry him says, 'Will you marry me?' He never says, 'Could you marry me?'

Women Talk Emotively, Men Are Literal

Because vocabulary is not a hotspot in a woman's brain, she can feel that the precise definition of words is irrelevant. She'll then take poetic licence with words, or won't shy away from exaggeration simply for effect. Men, however, interpret every word she says as if it is true and respond accordingly.

In an argument a man defines a woman's words to try to win. See if you recognise this exchange:

Robyn: 'You *never* agree with anything I say.'

John: 'What do you mean *never*? I agreed with your last two points didn't I?'

Robyn: 'You *always* disagree with me and you *always* want to be right!'

John: 'Not true! I don't *always* disagree with you! I agreed with you this morning, I agreed with you last night and I agreed with you last Saturday so you can't say I *always* disagree!'

Robyn: 'You say this *every* time I bring it up!'

John: 'That's a lie! I don't say it *every* time!'

Robyn: 'And you *only* ever touch me when you want sex!'

John: 'Stop exaggerating! I don't *only* ever ...'

She continues arguing, using emotions to fight him; he keeps defining her words. The argument escalates to the point where she refuses to talk or he stomps off to be on his own. But to argue successfully, a man needs to understand that a woman will use words that she doesn't really mean, so he shouldn't take them literally or define them. Take, for example, when a woman says, 'If I sat next to a woman who was wearing the identical dress, I'd just die! There's nothing worse!' She doesn't really mean that there is *nothing worse* or that she really expects to *die*, but a man's literal mind may respond with, 'No, you won't die, there are worse things than that!' which sounds sarcastic to a woman. By the same token, however, a woman needs to learn that she'll have to argue logically with a man if she wants to win and only give him one thought at a time. And women should never multi-track in an argument – their barbs have no chance of hitting home.

How Women Listen

Typically, a woman can use an average of six listening expressions in a ten-second period to reflect, and then feed back the speaker's emotions. Her face will mirror the emotions being expressed by the speaker. To someone watching, it can almost look as if the events being discussed are happening to both women.

Here is a typical ten-second sequence of a woman showing she is listening:

Sadness   Surprise   Anger   Joy   Fear   Desire

A woman reads the meaning of what is being said through voice intonation and the speaker's body language. This is exactly what a man needs to do to capture a woman's attention and keep her listening. Most men are daunted by the prospect of using facial feedback while listening, but it pays big dividends for the man who becomes adept at the art.

Men Listen Like Statues

The biological objective of our male warrior when listening was to remain impassive, so as not to betray his emotions.

Here is the same range of facial expressions used by a man in a ten-second listening period:

Sadness   Surprise   Anger   Joy   Fear   Desire

This is a light-hearted look at male listening technique, but recognising the truth in the humour gives it edge. This emotionless mask that men use while listening allows them to feel in control of the situation, but does not mean a man does not experience emotions. Brain scans reveal that men feel emotion as strongly as women, but avoid showing it.

How to Use the Grunt

Women use a range of high and low-pitched listening sounds (five tones) including 'oohs' and 'aahs', repeating a speakers' words or context, and multi-tracking the conversation. Men have a more restricted pitch range (three tones) and have difficulty decoding the meanings behind pitch changes, so speak in a more monotone voice.

To show that they are listening, men use what is called The Grunt – a series of short 'hmmps' with an occasional little nod of the head. Women criticise men for this form of listening, which partly explains why women accuse men of not listening. Often he *is* listening, he just doesn't look like he is. For businesswomen, there is money in The Grunt. If you're a woman explaining an idea or proposition to a man or men, it is vital that when a man is speaking, having his turn, you do not feed back his emotions, as you would with a woman. Just sit there expressionless, nod, grunt and don't interrupt. We have found that women who use this technique score big points on the credibility scale from men. Women who feed back men's emotions (or what they think the men's emotions might be) are heavily marked down on credibility and authority, and are sometimes described by men as 'dizzy' or 'too emotional'!

How to Get a Man to Listen

Make a time, give him an agenda, announce a time limit and tell him you don't want solutions or plans of action. Say, 'I'd like to talk with you about my day, Allan. Would after dinner be OK? I don't need any solutions to problems – I'd just like you to listen.' Most men will agree to a request like this because it has a time, a place and an objective – all the things that appeal to the male brain. And he is not expected to do any work.

The Schoolgirl Voice

Most women don't need a degree in evolutionary biology to know the power of talking in a high-pitched, almost singing voice. High voices are related to high oestrogen levels and their child-like quality appeals to most men's inbuilt urge to protect. Women prefer a deeper bass voice in a man as it is a powerful indicator of high testosterone levels, meaning greater virility. This drop to bass levels occurs in boys when they reach puberty as testosterone surges through their bodies and their voices 'break'. When a woman increases her speaking pitch and a man decreases his, it is a powerful signal that they are making a play for one another. We are not, in any way, implying that this is the way men and women *should* act around each other, but merely explaining what actually happens.

Think someone's giving you the come on? Listen to the pitch of his or her voice.

It is important to know that studies constantly show that, in business, a woman with a deeper voice is considered more intelligent, authoritative and credible. It is possible to practise a deeper voice by lowering the chin and speaking in a slower, more monotone way. In attempting to gain authority many women mistakenly raise their voice, which gives the impression that they are aggressive. Two interesting observations are that some overweight women use the 'girlie' voice to counteract the power of the large body size and others use it to encourage protective behaviour in men they like.

CHAPTER 5
SPATIAL ABILITY: MAPS, TARGETS AND PARALLEL PARKING

'Oh no! I can't believe this, girls ... Look at this map!
... I think we were supposed to turn right at that big
green mountain ...'

How a Map Almost Led to Divorce

Ray and Ruth were on their way to see a show in the city. Ray always drove. They never discussed why he always drove, he just did. And, like most men, he became a different person behind the wheel.

Ray asked Ruth to look up the address in the street directory. She opened it at the appropriate page and then turned the directory upside-down. She rotated it to the right way up and then turned it upside-down again. Then she sat silently and stared at it. She understood what a map meant but, when it came to applying it to where they were going, it seemed strangely irrelevant. It was like studying geography in school. All those pink and green shapes bore little resemblance to the real world in which she lived. Sometimes she coped with the map when they were heading North, but South was a disaster – and they were heading South. She rotated the map one more time. After several more seconds of silence, Ray spoke.

'Stop turning the map upside-down!' he snapped.

'But I need to face it in the direction we're going,' Ruth explained, meekly.

'Yeah, but you can't read it upside-down!' Ray barked.

'Look Ray, it makes logical sense to face the map in the direction we need to go. That way I can match the street signs with the directory!' she said, raising her voice indignantly.

'Yeah, but if the map was supposed to be read upside-down, they'd print the writing upside-down, right? Stop fooling around and tell me where to go!'

'I'll tell you where to go all right!' responded Ruth, furiously. She threw the street directory at him and shouted,

'Read it yourself!'

Does this argument sound familiar? It's one of the most common between men and women of all races, stretching back thousands of years. In the 11th Century, Lady Godiva rode her horse naked down the wrong Coventry street, Juliet got lost trying to get back home after a love tryst with Romeo, Cleopatra threatened Marc Antony with castration for trying to force her to understand his battle maps and the Wicked Witch of the West often headed South, North or East.

Sexist Thinking

Reading maps and understanding where you are relies on spatial ability. Brain scans show that spatial ability is located mostly in the right brain for men and boys, and is one of a male's strongest abilities. It developed from ancient times to allow men, the hunters, to calculate the speed, movement and distance of prey, work out how fast they had to run to catch their targets, and know how much force they needed to kill their lunch with a rock or a spear. Spatial ability is located in both brain hemispheres for women but does not have a specific measurable location as it does in males. Only about 10% of women have spatial abilities that are as dynamic as those of the best men.

The majority of women

have limited spatial ability.

To some people, this research may appear sexist because we will be discussing the kind of strengths and abilities at which males excel, and the pursuits and occupations in which biology has given them the clear advantage. Later, however, we will look at areas where women have the upper hand.

The Lunch-Chaser in Action

Spatial ability means being able to picture in the mind the shape of things, their dimensions, co-ordinates, proportions, movement and geography. It also involves being able to imagine an object being rotated in space, navigating around an obstacle course and seeing things from a three-dimensional perspective. Its purpose is to work out the movement of a target and know how to hit it.

Iowa State University professor of psychology Dr Camilla Benbow scanned the brains of more than a million boys and girls to study their spatial ability and reported that differences between the sexes were already striking by the age of four. She found that while girls were excellent at seeing two dimensions in the brain, boys had the ability to see a third dimension, giving depth. On three-dimensional video tests, boys outstripped girls in spatial ability by a ratio of 4:1 and the best girls were often outclassed by the lowest scoring boys. With males, this is a specific brain function located in at least four sites in the right front hemisphere and several smaller areas in the left.

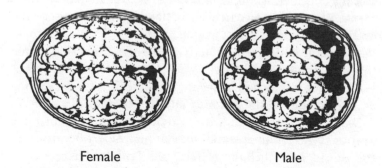

Female   Male

Location of spatial ability in the brain. (Black areas represent activity.) Institute of Psychiatry, London, 1999.

Not having a specific location for spatial ability means that most women generally score on the low side with spatial tasks. Most women don't enjoy spatial activities and don't pursue careers or pastimes that require them.

Having a specific area for spatial ability, most men and boys are good at any activities that use those skills and often pursue related careers and sports. For males, it's also the area of the brain that allows them to solve problems. Spatial ability is not strong in women and girls because being able to chase animals and find the way home was never part of woman's job description. This is why many women have trouble reading a map or street directory.

Women don't have good

spatial skills because they evolved

chasing little else besides men.

There are thousands of documented scientific studies that confirm male superiority in spatial skills. This is not surprising considering his evolution as a hunter. But modern man no longer has to catch lunch. Today, he uses his spatial ability in other areas such as golf, computer games, football, hunting and any sport or activity involving chasing something or aiming at a target. Most women think hunting is boring. But if they had a specific right brain area for aiming at a target they would not only enjoy it, they would succeed.

Men are so obsessed with watching another man hit a ball at a target that some of the highest-paid people in the world now include golfers, footballers, basketballers and tennis players. You don't need a college degree to be respected any more; you simply need to be good at estimating speed, distance, angles and directions.

Why Men Know Where to Go

Spatial ability allows a man to rotate a map in his mind and know in which direction to go. If he has to return to the same location at a later time, he doesn't need the map, as his spatial area can store the information. Most males can read a map while facing North and know that they need to go South. Similarly, most males can read a map and then successfully navigate by memory. Studies show that a man's brain measures speed and distance to know when to change direction. Most men, if put in an unfamiliar room with no windows, can point North. As a lunch-chaser, he needed to find his way back home or there would be little chance of survival.

Most men can always point north, even

if they have no idea where they are.

Sit in any sports stadium and you can witness how men leave their seats to buy a drink and successfully navigate their way back to that seat some time later. Go to any city in the world and watch female tourists standing at junctions furiously turning their maps around and looking lost. Visit a multi-storey car park at any shopping mall and watch female shoppers wandering gloomily around trying to find their cars.

Why Boys Hang Out in Video Arcades

Visit any video or pinball arcade in the world and you'll see that it's full of teenage boys using their spatial skills. Let's look at some of the scientific studies highlighting spatial ability. Most of them involved the assembly of three-dimensional mechanical apparatus.

A study at Yale University found that only 22% of females could perform such tasks as well as males. It also discovered that while 68% of males could programme a VCR or similar equipment from a set of written instructions on the first attempt, only 16% of females could do it. Boys excelled when their right eye was covered so that only the left eye could receive information which was fed to the right brain where most spatial skills are located. It made no difference to girls which eye they used, because their brain tried to solve the problems using both sides. This is why women rarely choose to be motor mechanics, engineers or airline pilots.

Dr Camilla Benbow and colleague Dr Julian Stanley tested a group of gifted children and found that boys good at maths outnumbered girls by 13 to 1. Boys can construct a block building from two-dimensional plans easier and quicker than girls, they can estimate angles accurately and can see whether a flat surface is level. These ancient hunting skills are the reason men dominate areas like architecture, chemistry, building, and statistics. Boys test better in hand–eye co-ordination, making them more proficient at ball sports. This accounts for the male obsession with cricket, golf, football, basketball or any game that involves estimating co-ordinates and throwing, chasing or shooting at a target. It also explains why video and pinball arcades and skateboard rinks around the world are full of boys but there are few girls. Most of the girls are there to impress the boys but, as most teenage girls quickly learn, the boys are more obsessed with the games than they are in noticing them.

In 1999 Dr Sandra Witelson led a team of scientists at McMaster University in Ontario, Canada, which analysed the anatomy of Albert Einstein's brain and compared it to the preserved brains of 35 men and 56 women known to have normal intelligence when they died. They also compared his brain to those of eight other men who were of similar age to Einstein when they died. They found that the spatial area of his brain, related to his mathematical reasoning, was 15 percent wider on both sides than in normal men and women.

Boys' Brains Develop Differently

Parents who have both sons and daughters quickly come to realise that boys are very different to girls in their speed of development. The right brain in boys develops and grows at a faster rate than the left brain. It develops more connections within itself and also has fewer connections with the left brain. In girls, both sides grow at a more balanced speed giving girls a better range of abilities. Since they also have more connections between left and right through a thicker corpus callosum, there tends to be more ambidextrous girls than boys, and many more women who have difficulty in knowing their left hand from their right.

Testosterone hormones inhibit the left brain growth in boys as a trade-off for greater right side development, giving them a better spatial ability for hunting. Studies of children between the ages of five and eighteen show that boys outstrip girls in their ability to move a beam of light to hit a target, reproduce a pattern by walking it out on the floor, assemble a range of three-dimensional objects and solve problems requiring mathematical reasoning. All of these skills are located mainly in the right brain of at least 80% of men and boys.

Diana and her Furniture

When the removal van was unloading the furniture to go into Diana's new home, she was busily running her tape measure over every piece to see if it would fit into certain places. As she measured the dining room dresser, her 14-year-old son Cliff said, 'Forget it mum – that won't fit where you want it to go. It's too big.' Diana then measured the space and Cliff was right. She could not comprehend how he could look at a piece of furniture and imagine whether or not it would fit into a space in the house. And how did he do it? He used his spatial ability.

Testing Spatial Ability

American scientist Dr D. Wechsler created a series of IQ Tests that eliminated sexual bias against men or women during spatial tests. By testing members of cultures from primitive races to sophisticated city dwellers all over the world, he, like other researchers elsewhere, came to the conclusion that women had superiority over men in general intelligence, being around three per cent more intelligent than men, despite having slightly smaller brains. When it came to solving maze puzzles, however, men were overwhelmingly superior to women, scoring 92% of the top honours against women's eight per cent, regardless of culture. Critics might say this proves women are too intelligent to play silly maze puzzles, but it does graphically demonstrate male spatial ability.

The following spatial test was developed at the University of Plymouth and is the type used as an occupational test in the selection of pilots, navigators and air traffic controllers. It measures your ability to take two-dimensional information and construct, in your mind, a three-dimensional object.

Imagine that the puzzle in Test 1 is an opened-up cube. Assuming that the face with the cross x is on the right and the circle is on the left, which of your options A, B, C or D is the correct one? Do the test now.

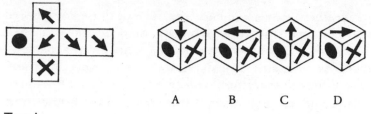

A   B   C   D

Test 1

This test requires your brain to imagine the image in three dimensions and then rotate it to get the correct angle. These are the same skills required to read a map or street directory, land a plane or chase a buffalo. (The correct answer is A.)

Now here's a more complex version of the test that requires your brain to make even more spatial rotations.

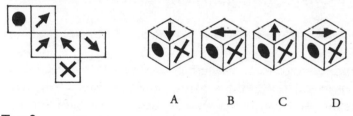

A   B   C   D

Test 2

Tests by zoologists show that male mammals are superior to female mammals in spatial abilities – male rats are far better at finding their way out of mazes than female rats, and male elephants are better than females at relocating a waterhole. (By the way, the correct answer for Test 2 is C.)

How Women Can Navigate

'If men didn't design maps that way, we wouldn't have to turn them upside down,' many women complain. The British Cartography Society, however, reports that 50% of its members are female and that 50% of those who design and edit maps are also women. 'Map design is a two-dimensional task in which women are equally as capable as men,' said leading British cartographer Alan Collinson. 'The difficulty that most women have is reading and navigating with the map because they need a three-dimensional perspective to navigate a route. I design tourist maps that have a three-dimensional perspective – they show trees, mountains and other landmarks. Women have much greater success with this type of map. Our tests show that men have the ability to turn a two-dimensional map into a three-dimensional view in their mind, but most women don't seem to be able to do this.'

Women dramatically improve their navigational skills using perspective maps.

Another interesting finding has been that men score highly when navigating with a group leader who verbally tells them new directions at each point on a given route. Women, by contrast, perform abysmally when given verbal instructions. This shows how men can convert sound signals into three-dimensional mind maps to visualise the correct direction and route to take, whereas women perform better with a three-dimensional perspective map.

What if You Can't Find North?

Australian sailor Kay Cottee was the first woman to single-handedly circumnavigate the world non-stop. This is clearly a woman who knew where she was going, right?

At a recent conference she told us that she had difficulty reading a street directory. Stunned, we asked, 'So how did you go around the world?' 'That's navigation,' Kay replied. 'You programme the computer and it takes you in the right direction. I don't go out to sea and say, 'Gee I think I should turn left ...' A street directory is an intuitive thing. You need to 'feel' which way to go. When I go to a strange city I always catch taxis to get around. I tried rental cars but I always ended up going the wrong way.'

People find it hard to believe that Kay Cottee could get lost trying to find her boat to circumnavigate the world but she clearly shows how, with determination, planning and courage, you can navigate your way around the world – even if you can't read a street directory – by organising the right people and equipment needed to achieve the task.

The Flying Map

We (the authors) travel the world for nine months of the year giving seminars, and spend much of our time in hire cars. Allan normally drives as his spatial skills are better than Barbara's which leaves her to navigate. Barbara has almost no navigational ability so she and Allan have argued and fought their way around the world for years – from city to city, country to country. Allan has had street directories and maps thrown at him in practically every language by Barbara, and on several occasions she has fled from him and his maps, catching buses or trains and shouting, 'Read it yourself!'

Barbara has no sense of direction, but

Allan can never find socks in his drawer.

Fortunately, their research into spatial ability alerted them to the problems that arise when one partner has little spatial ability and the other does not understand this. Today, Allan reads the map before driving and Barbara talks and points out interesting features of the landscape that Allan normally misses. They are still happily married and flying maps no longer pose a hazard to passing motorists.

The Upside-Down Map

In England in 1998, John and Ashley Sims created a two-way map that has a standard map view when travelling North and a second, upside-down view, with South at the top of the page, for travelling South. In a British national newspaper's weekend magazine they offered a free map to the first 100 people who wrote in. They received requests from more than 15,000 women – and a handful of men. They told us that men saw no point in an Upside-Down Map or thought it was a joke. Women, however, are impressed because it replaces the need for spatial rotation.

BMW motor cars were the first to install Global Positioning System (GPS) visual navigational equipment in their vehicles which allows the image to be turned upside down to match the direction the car is travelling. Predictably, it has proved a huge hit with women.

A Final Test

Try this test developed by human resource and research company Saville and Holdsworth (UK) Ltd which is given to candidates to test their spatial reasoning for jobs such as air traffic controllers. If you can't do it in under three minutes, you're out. This is even harder than the first two and, if you're male, should increase the temperature of your right hemisphere.

In this test, you are given a pattern which, if cut out, could be folded to make a three-dimensional box. You must decide which, if any, of the four boxes in each set could be made by folding the pattern, and show this by circling the appropriate one. If you think that none of the boxes could be made from the pattern, do not circle any box.

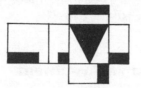

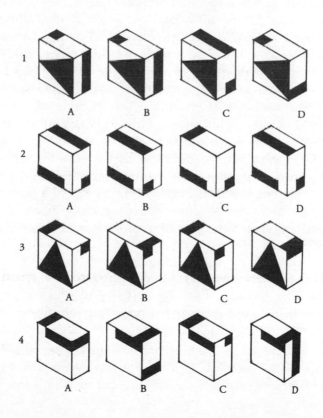

Most people who successfully complete this test in under three minutes are men, particularly those with three-dimensional jobs like architects and mathematicians. Now you know why 94% of air traffic controllers are men. Most women think these type of tests are a waste of time, although we found one woman who completed it successfully in nine seconds. Her occupation? She's an actuary. (The answers are 1B, 2D, 3C, none.)

How to Avoid an Argument

Men love to drive fast around winding roads because their spatial skills come into play – gear ratios, clutch and brake combinations, relative speed to corners, angles and distances. And they do it with the radio turned off.

The modern male driver sits behind the wheel, hands his wife a map and asks her to navigate. With limited spatial ability she becomes silent and starts turning the map around and feels incompetent. Then she tries to identify something on the horizon that resembles something on the map. Most men don't understand that if you don't have specific areas in the brain for mental map rotation, you'll rotate it in your hands. It makes perfect sense to a woman to face a map in the direction she is travelling. For a man to avoid arguments, he should avoid asking a woman to read a map.

To have a happy life: Never insist that a

woman read a map or street directory.

Having spatial ability on both sides of the brain interferes with a female's speech function, so if you give a woman a street directory, she'll stop talking before she turns it around. Give it to a man and he'll continue talking – but he'll also turn the radio off because he can't operate his hearing functions at the same time as his map-reading skills. That's why when a phone rings in his home he demands that everyone keeps quiet while he answers it.

Women work out mathematical problems mainly in the left side of the brain which not only makes them slower at calculus but explains why so many women and girls perform mathematical functions aloud. Men everywhere shout, 'Would you mind calculating in your head please! I can't concentrate!' as they try to read their newspapers.

How to Argue While Driving

A husband who teaches his wife to drive is heading for the divorce courts. Men all around the world give the same instructions to women: 'Turn left – slow down! – change gears – watch out for those pedestrians – concentrate – stop crying!' For a man, driving is a test of his spatial ability relative to the environment. For a woman, the purpose of driving is to get safely from point A to point B. A man's best strategy as a passenger is to close his eyes, turn up the radio and stop commentating because, overall, women are safer drivers than men. She'll get him there – it may just take a little longer, that's all. But at least he can relax and arrive alive.

A woman will criticise a man's driving because his spatial ability allows him to make decisions and judgements that look dangerous to her. Provided he doesn't have a poor driving record, she also needs to relax and not criticise, and just let him do the driving. When the first drop of rain hits the windscreen, a woman immediately turns on the wipers, something men can never understand. A man's brain waits until the exact amount of raindrops are on the screen relative to the speed of the wipers and he turns the wipers on when the precise amount of time has passed. In other words, he uses spatial ability.

How to Sell to a Woman

Never give a woman directions like, 'Head North' or 'Go West for five kilometres' as this requires compass skills. Instead, give directions involving landmarks such as, 'Drive past McDonald's and head for the building with the National Bank sign on top.' This allows a woman to pick up these landmarks with her peripheral vision. Builders and architects everywhere lose millions in business deals by presenting two-dimensional plans and blueprints to female decision-makers. A man's brain can convert the plan to three dimensions to see how the building would look completed, but to a woman it's just a page of irrelevant lines. A three-dimensional model or computer image will sell houses to women. With this information, a woman need never again feel like an idiot when looking at a map. Give it to a man, it's *his* job.

It's much more relaxing for a man to navigate and drive while a woman talks about the interesting landmarks and sights along the way. As you know, a man has inferior verbal skills compared to a woman, so his navigational skills seem like a fair trade-off. It means that he can find his way to the address of his new girlfriend, even if he won't know what to say when he gets there.

The Pain of Reverse Parallel Parking

If you were asked to look at cars that had been reverse parked in a street, could you tell which cars had been parked by men and which by women? Research commissioned by an English defensive driving school showed that men in the UK averaged 82% accuracy in reverse parking someone else's car close to the kerb and 71% could successfully park their vehicle on the first attempt. Women scored only 22% accuracy, while a mere 23% could do it successfully on the first attempt. A similar study in Singapore gave men an accuracy score of 66%, with 68% doing it first time. For women, the accuracy result was 19%, and only 12% did it the first time. The bottom line: if the driver is a Singaporean woman, get out of the way! The best parkers are German men with 88% doing it successfully on the first attempt. Parking tests at driving schools show that women generally do better at reverse parking than men during driver training, but statistics show women perform worse in real life situations. This is because women are better than men at learning a task and successfully repeating it, provided the environment and conditions under which they do it don't change. In traffic, however, every situation presents a new set of data to be assessed and men's spatial ability is better suited to handle this task.

Most women would prefer to park the car in a larger space somewhere else and walk back to their destination rather than reverse park into a tight spot.

If women ran local councils, reverse and parallel parking would be banned!

In recent times many regional towns and cities have introduced 45-degree rear-to-kerb reverse parking because it has been shown to be safer by allowing the driver to drive forward when they depart. Unfortunately, this has not helped most women's concerns about reverse parking as it still requires spatial abilities to estimate angles and distances.

We surveyed 20 local councils who implemented this type of reverse parking and discovered that there were practically no women involved in the decision. It was almost always men. If a council was made up completely of women, reverse and parallel parking would no longer be allowed! They would arrange for drive-through style parking that eliminates the need for reversing or estimating angles and distances. This would take up a greater amount of space, but there would be fewer accidents.

Women Are Safer Drivers

A study of the insurance records of 2.3 million UK drivers in the year 2000 revealed that 25.5% of women drivers had made a claim in the last 4 years compared to 18.6% of men. It also showed that 9% of women drivers do not have a no-claim bonus – indicating that they had an accident in the past 12 months – compared to 6.5% of men. It would be easy to conclude that women are worse drivers than men are but closer examination shows a different story. Women are more cautious drivers, they will take an extra couple of seconds before moving off on a roundabout or wait when there is nothing to wait for. This caution can lead to more accidents because other drivers become frustrated at what seems like indecision. Women have more accidents but their insurance payouts are lower because it involved more bumps and scrapes. Most high payout claims and total write-offs involve male drivers with too much testosterone on the pedal. Women make more claims but men are more dangerous drivers. The study also found that divorced women are more likely to have smashes than married women.

How Women Were Misled

So where does all this spatial evidence leave women? Many well-intentioned groups were convinced that once they were freed from the supposed chains of male oppression and prejudice, they would quickly climb to the top levels of most male-dominated professions and pastimes. But, as you are about to see, men continue to hold a virtual monopoly in those professions and pursuits that require spatial ability. Millions of women have ignored their natural inclinations towards careers and pursuits in which they could naturally excel with their particular brain-oriented skills.

Spatial Ability in Education

As we've seen, our biology directs us to occupations and pastimes that are compatible with the wiring of our brain. Let's analyse one area where equal opportunity is a high priority – teaching. We interviewed education officials in Australia, New Zealand and Britain who all emphasised that they try to keep the split of male/female teachers at 50/50 to give equal opportunity to the sexes. In Britain in 1999, 48% of teachers were male and 52% female. The feminised brain is better suited to teaching than the male brain because its communication and human interaction abilities are more highly developed. Let's look at what subject preferences are selected by teachers of each sex.

Subject	Number of Teachers	% Men	% Women
Biology	5,100	49	51
Business studies	6,400	50	50
History	13,800	54	46
Geography	14,200	56	44
Social studies	11,000	52	48
Music	5,600	51	49
Careers education	1,900	47	53
Personal and Social education	74,200	47	53
General studies	7,900	53	47
Classics	510	47	53
Physical education	20,100	58	42
Religious education	13,400	56	44
Art	9,400	44	56

There are two lessons to be learnt from this table. Firstly, the subjects taught are those that don't require a high degree of left or right brain dominance to be able to teach them. A high degree of spatial ability is not required and neither is great left brain verbal capability. You can see that the percentages are spread fairly evenly between male and female teachers.

Subject	Number of Teachers	%Men	%Women
Physics	4,400	82	18
Info Technology	10,700	69	31
Sciences	28,900	65	35
Chemistry	4,600	62	38

Subjects requiring spatial ability

The above table shows clearly that where the ability to think spatially is a necessity, men dominate.

Spatial Skill Occupations

Following is a list of occupations where high spatial ability is critical to job performance and in which someone's life can be lost if it's absent. You don't need to be a rocket scientist to understand the significance of this chart and its relationship to male right-brain hunting skills.

Those determined to cling on to the belief that natural abilities count for nought still claim that male oppression, men's 'boys only' attitudes and traditionally male-biased unions have prevented women from achieving equality in these professions. The Royal Institute of British Architects, however, reports that 50% of students enrolling in architecture courses are women, but that they only account for nine per cent of all practising architects. Obviously, some of the women who did not become architects chose parenthood, but what happened to the rest? In accountancy, 17% of British accountants are women yet 38% of all those who started the course were women.

'Why aren't there more female airline pilots?' we asked the airlines. 'They don't take the course,' was the answer. 'Women aren't interested in flying planes.' Most airline officials were vague about, or unaware of, the significance of spatial ability in flying and many were nervous about making any comment on gender differences despite the glaringly obvious fact that 98% of all cockpit crews are male. One thing is clear here: women are not in most of these professions because they don't enrol in the courses. Their brain bias is not suited to these areas so they are not interested in learning to do the job.

Occupation	% Men
Flight engineer	100.0%
Engineer	100.0%
Racing driver	99.8%
Nuclear engineer	98.3%
Pilot	99.2%
Air traffic control	94.0%
Dragcar/bike racer	93.6%
Architect	91.0%
Flight deck officer	90.5%
Actuary	90.0%
Billiards	87.0%
Accountant	83.0%

Billiards and Nuclear Science

In the course of our research, we spoke with a number of professional snooker and billiards players. 'The women who play professional billiards think and act like men,' said one former world champion. 'They talk like us and dress like us too – suits and bow-ties.' The female players, however, believed that if they practised as much as the men, they'd be just as capable. Many felt that men's attitudes towards them was a significant factor in holding them back. 'But what about spatial ability?' we asked. 'Measuring the relative speed and angles of the balls, the distances to the pocket and final placement of the white ball?' 'Never heard of it,' was the answer. Again, men's attitudes were held responsible for the overall lack of female champions and participants.

'We offer equal opportunity to both sexes,' the Institute of Nuclear Engineers told us, 'but we hire based on capability, not equality.' And 98.3% of nuclear engineers are males. Interestingly, the Institute's research found that female engineers are more capable with letters of the alphabet than men, and that men are better with numbers. This makes sense – letters are linked to people, relationships and verbal abilities but numbers relate to the spatial relationship between things.

Look at history and you will see that practically no women have excelled in areas where spatial ability and mathematical reasoning are required, such as chess, composing and rocket science. Some may claim that sexist male tyranny has kept women out of these pursuits, but look around and you'll see that in our world of equal opportunity, the women who eclipse men in spatially related pursuits are rare. The main reason is that their brains tell them they're more interested in defending their nests rather than attacking someone else's.

Women excel in the creative areas such as performing arts, teaching, human resources and literature, all fields where abstract reasoning is not paramount. While men play chess, women dance and decorate.

The Computer Industry

Computer science is built largely on mathematics, which relies on spatial ability and, as a result, it's a male domain. Some computer science areas, however, such as programming or user-interface design, require more understanding of human psychology than mathematics and these are the areas which have the highest numbers of women.

Results of a survey in *US Business Women In Computing* magazine show a steady decline in the number of women entering the information technology workplace between 1995 and 2000, and cites the reason as a lack of interest from women in taking these courses. The study also found that women are twice as likely as men to use computers in the workplace. While 84% of women saw the computer simply as a means to an end or as a tool to provide creative freedom, only 33% of men shared this view. The survey showed that 67% of men saw the technology or playing with the programmes and accessories as more important in computing, in common with just 16% of women.

Maths and Accounting

The males who enter spatially-related occupations and professions usually remain and dominate. Most maths teachers are still males even though, in this subject area, the gender gap is closing. In the year 2000, 58% of maths teachers in the United Kingdom were men.

So how do we explain the increasing percentage of women teaching this subject? The likely explanation is that women are more suited to teaching, interaction and organising groups, and are more committed to learning the basics than men. Because they are teaching the same material over and over again, they can do an excellent job with teaching most subjects, including maths. This would also explain why in the field of accountancy there is a general increase in the number of female accountants. Accounting has become a customer-friendly sales role for which women's brains are better suited, with the accounting function becoming secondary. In large accounting firms everywhere it is now common to see a female accountant wooing and winning the clients and the mathematical accounting work delegated to the junior males in the back room. When the requirement for the job is pure spatial ability and mathematical reasoning, however, men still dominate. This is why 91% of actuaries and 99% of all engineers are male.

All Things Being Equal ...

In Australia, just five percent of the engineering workforce is female yet, on average, they earn 14% more than their male counterparts. This indicates that where equal spatial ability exists, women can perform at a higher level than men. In professional motor-racing there has been almost no female champions since the invention of the motor car but in drag-racing, around 10% of the participants and winners are women. Why? Drag-racing does not require the spatial skills to deal with speeds, angles, corners, overtaking and complicated gear ratios. Drag-racers drive in a straight line and the winner is the person who has the fastest reaction time to the green light – an advantage that women have over men.

Where equal spatial ability exists, women

can perform at a higher level than men.

Although most female drag-racers we tested on the Brain-Wiring Test showed overall higher male brain orientation than non-racing women, they still spoke of the benefits in drag-racing as relationship-orientated. 'The guys are really great to work with,' they said. 'Everyone pitches in.' And, 'We're all good friends.' The male drivers saw the benefits as winning trophies, having wonderful car specifications and bragging about accidents they had survived.

Boys and their Toys

Boys love their toys. This is why 99% of all patents are registered by men. Girls love to play with toys too but usually lose interest by age 12 as they begin to grow into young women. Men never lose their obsession for impractical, spatially-related toys – they just spend a lot more on them. They love miniature pocket TVs, mobile phones shaped like cars, computer and video games, digital cameras, complicated gadgets, lights that go off or on by voice command and anything that has an engine. If it beeps, blinks and needs at least six D-cell batteries, most men want one.

How Women Feel

Any discussion on gender differences such as those in this book brings howls of protest from feminists and politically correct activists, who see it as undermining many of their arguments for a fair go in life. But while the prejudices of society may reinforce and exacerbate stereotypical behaviour in males and females, and fundamental inequities, the stereotypes are not the cause of the behaviour. Our basic biology and how our brains are organised are the culprits. Many women feel that they are failures or that women in general have failed by not conquering male-dominated areas. That's simply not true. Women haven't failed; they've merely not been particularly well-equipped to enter areas that suit male brains much more.

Women haven't failed – they've

only failed to be like men.

The idea that women have not succeeded in society is only valid when based on the assumption that success by male standards is, or should be, the benchmark for everyone's success. But who says being a chief executive controlling a corporation, flying a jumbo jet or programming a space shuttle's computer is the ultimate measure of fulfilment?

Men do. It's *their* standard of excellence, not everyone's.

Can You Improve Your Spatial Skill?

In a word, yes. There are several alternatives. You can wait for the natural process of evolution to take place and constantly practise your spatial activities until your brain develops sufficient connections. Be prepared for the long haul with this one, though. Biologists estimate that it could take thousands of years.

A course of testosterone hormones will also improve spatial ability, but this is not a satisfactory option as the downside includes increased aggression level, baldness and a beard, which might not suit most women.

It is now clear that practice and repetition help permanently to create more brain connections for a given task. Rats raised in cages full of toys have more brain mass than rats with no toys. Humans who retire to do nothing lose their brain mass, whereas those who keep active mental interests maintain mass and even increase it. Learning and practising how maps work can greatly increase your practical ability to use them, just as daily practice on the piano makes for more competent playing. Unless the player has the kind of brain circuitry that facilitates intuitive playing, however, lots of regular practice is required to maintain a reasonable level. Unless the piano player or map reader keeps that up, their skill level will diminish more quickly and take longer to recover than a person whose brain is wired to handle the task.

A bald head and a beard might

be too high a price to pay for

women to improve their spatial skills.

You can successfully teach a dog to walk on its hind legs, and if it repeats this behaviour regularly, its offspring are also likely to do it too. But it's not a dog's *natural* position and it takes a lot of pain and effort to walk that way. A dog's natural position is on *four* legs.

Some Useful Strategies

If you are a woman raising a son or have men in your life, you need to understand that while they have excellent spatial ability, most can still only do one thing at a time. Most need help to organise their homework, diary and life in order to be effective boys and men. These organisational skills come more naturally to girls and women. Albert Einstein was a spatial genius but he didn't speak until the age of five and he had almost no organisational or interpersonal skills, as his hairstyle showed.

If you are a male in a spatially-related job such as building or architecture, you need to understand that most women need a three-dimensional perspective if you are to be convincing.

Want to persuade a woman to go with a certain set of plans? Show her a three-dimensional version.

If you are recruiting women into spatially-related occupations such as engineering, the market for these prospects is only about 10% of all women, so target only those women. To attempt a marketing strategy to encompass all women based on the fact that they make up 50% of the population is a futile exercise.

In Summary

Ray and Ruth now get on well when they travel together. He decides which route they will take and he navigates. She talks and points out landmarks and he listens, without interruption. She no longer criticises his driving because she knows that his spatial ability lets him take what she may consider a risk, but to him is perfectly safe driving.

Ray bought a camera worth $3,000 with all types of spatially-related gadgetry and Ruth now understands why he loves it. When it's her turn to take a photograph, he sets everything up for her and shows her how to take a good shot instead of laughing when she can't work out how to turn it on.

When men stop asking women to navigate, everyone's lives will be happier, and when women stop criticising men's driving ability, there will be far fewer arguments. We are all good at different things so, if you are not good at a particular task, don't worry about it. You can improve with practice but don't let it ruin your life. Or that of your partner.

CHAPTER 6
THOUGHTS, ATTITUDES, EMOTIONS AND OTHER DISASTER AREAS

Colin and Jill were driving to a party in an unfamiliar area. According to the directions, it should have taken them 20 minutes. It had already taken them 50, and there was still no sign of their destination. Colin was becoming grumpy and Jill started feeling despondent as they passed the same garage for the third time.

Jill: 'Darling, I think we should have turned right at the garage. Let's stop and ask directions.'

Colin: 'There's no problem. I know it's around here somewhere ...'

Jill: 'But we're half-an-hour late already and the party's started – let's stop and ask someone!'

Colin: 'Listen, I know what I'm doing! Do you want to drive or are you going to let me?'

Jill: 'No, I don't want to drive, but I don't want to go round and round in circles all night either!'

Colin: 'OK then, why don't I just turn the car around and we'll go back home!'

Most men and women will recognise this conversation. A woman can't understand why this wonderful man she loves so much suddenly turns into Mad Max on steroids just because he's lost. If she was lost, she'd ask for directions, so what's his problem? Why can't he just admit he doesn't know?

Why did Moses spend 40 years wandering in the desert?

He refused to ask for directions.

Women don't mind admitting mistakes because, in their world, it's seen as a form of bonding and building trust. The last man to admit he'd made a mistake, however, was General Custer.

Our Different Perceptions

Men and women perceive the same world through different eyes. A man sees things and objects and their relationship to each other in a spatial way, as though he was putting the pieces of a jigsaw puzzle together. Women literally take in a bigger, wider picture and see the fine detail, but the individual pieces of the puzzles and their relationship to the next piece is more relevant than their spatial positioning.

Male awareness is concerned with getting results, achieving goals, status and power, beating the competition and getting efficiently to the bottom line. Female awareness is focused on communication, co-operation, harmony, love, sharing and our relationship to one another. This contrast is so great that it's amazing men and women can even consider living together in the first place.

Boys Like Things, Girls Like People

Girls' brains are wired to respond to people and faces but boys' brains respond to objects and their shapes. Studies of babies from a few hours old to a few months all show this one clear point: boys like things, girls like people. Scientific, measurable differences between the sexes show how each perceives the same world through the bias of their differently wired brains. Baby girls are attracted to faces and maintain eye contact two to three times longer than boys, and baby boys are more interested in watching the movement of a mobile with irregular shapes and patterns.

At 12 weeks old, girls can distinguish pictures of family from strangers, while boys cannot, but boys are better at relocating a lost toy. These differences are obvious, long before social conditioning has had a chance to take effect. Pre-school children were tested with a pair of binocular eye-viewers that showed objects to one eye and people's faces to the other eye. The tests of the children's recall showed that girls remembered people and their emotions and boys recalled more about things and their shapes. At school, girls sit in circles, talking and each mirroring the group's body language. You cannot identify a leader.

Girls want relationships and co-operation, boys want power and status.

If a girl builds something, it is usually a long, low-profile building with the emphasis on the imaginary people who are in the building, whereas boys compete to build a bigger and higher structure than the next boy. Boys run, jump, wrestle and pretend they are aeroplanes or tanks, while girls talk about which boys they like or how stupid some of the boys look. At pre-school, a new girl is welcomed by other girls and they all know each other's names. A new boy is usually treated indifferently by other boys and is only included in the group if the hierarchy feels he can serve a useful purpose. At the end of the day, most boys would not know the new boy's name or details, but they'd know how good or bad a player he was. Girls welcome and accept others and are even more sympathetic to someone who may have a handicap or disability, but boys are likely to ostracise or victimise the disadvantaged person.

Despite the best intentions of parents to raise boys and girls in the same way, brain differences finally decide preferences and behaviour. Give a four-year-old girl a teddy bear or toy and she'll make it her best friend; give it to a boy and he'll dismember it to see how it works, leave it in pieces and then move on to the next.

Boys are interested in things and how they work, girls are interested in people and relationships. When adults reminisce about weddings, women talk about the ceremony and the people who attended, men talk about the 'stag night'.

Boys Compete, Girls Co-operate

Girls' groups are co-operative and you cannot visually identify a leader. Girls use talk to show their level of bonding and each girl usually has a best friend with whom to share secrets. Girls will ostracise a girl who exerts authority by saying, 'She thinks she's somebody' or they call her 'bossy'. Boys' groups have a hierarchy with leaders who can be identified by their superior or assertive talk and body language, and each boy hustles for status in the group. Power and status are all-important in a boy's group. This is usually achieved through a boy's skills or knowledge or by his ability to talk tough to others or fight off challengers. Girls are happy to build relationships with teachers and friends while boys question teachers and prefer to explore the spatial relationships of the world, and to do so alone.

What We Talk About

Listen to any group of men, women, boys or girls in any country and you'll hear how the brain circuitry of each sex causes them to talk about the same things differently. Girls talk about who likes who or who is angry with who. They play in small groups and share 'secrets' about others as a form of bonding. As teenagers, girls talk about boys, weight, clothes and their friends. As adults, women talk about diet, personal relationships, marriage, children, lovers, personalities, clothes, the actions of others, work relationships and anything to do with people and personal issues. Boys talk about things and activities – who did what, who is good at something and how things work. As teenagers, they talk about sports, mechanics and the function of things. As men they discuss sports, their work, news, what they did or where they went, technology, cars and mechanical gadgets.

A 1999 survey of 1,000 telephone users by the British cable phone company Telewest revealed what men and women talk about on the telephone.

	Men	Women
Friends	30%	53%
Sex/relationships	18%	22%
Work	25%	11%
Sports	16%	2%
Other	11%	12%

A third of all women said their calls lasted at least 15 minutes and half the men said their calls were less than 5 minutes.

Talking Dirty

Women have always assumed that men huddle in groups for sleazy sex chats, but that isn't true. If a man, in the company of other men, actually began to talk about what he had done in bed the night before, including operational details, his companions would become speechless or leave. This is not because he is ruining a woman's reputation, but because the speaker might produce statistics, including times and centimetres, that the other men would have difficulty in meeting. This is why men prefer to joke about sex.

While men have side-by-side friendships based on things and achievement, women have face-to-face friendships based on emotional sharing. That's why women's arguments can be so hurtful – they know more personal details about each other and have more ammunition to hurl. Women are never withholding when it comes to sex talk either. They freely discuss techniques, strategies, times and sizes. And they are graphic in their descriptions.

What Modern Men and Women Want

A recent study conducted in five Western countries asked men and women to describe the kind of person they would ideally like to be. Men overwhelmingly chose adjectives including *bold, competitive, capable, dominant, assertive, admired* and *practical*. From the same list women chose *warm, loving, generous, sympathetic, attractive, friendly* and *giving*. Women rated being of service to others and meeting interesting people as high on their scale of values, whereas men rated prestige, power and owning things as important. Men valued things, women valued relationships. The structure of their brains dictated their preferences.

Emotion in the Brain

Canadian research scientist Sandra Witleson conducted tests on men and women to locate the position of emotion in the brain. Using emotionally-charged images that were shown first to the right hemisphere via the left eye and ear and then to the left hemisphere via the right eye and ear. From MRI scans, she concluded that men's emotion is located mainly in two areas in the right hemisphere, and women's is located throughout both hemispheres. New research indicates that our emotions may be located in various organs in the body in amino acids called neuropeptides and that these areas revealed in brain scans are simply remote controls for these neuropeptides.

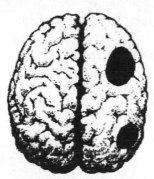 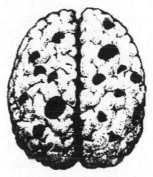

Emotion in men   Emotion in women

For men, emotion is generally positioned in the right brain, meaning that it can operate separately from other brain functions. For example, in an argument, a man can argue logic and words (left brain) and then switch to spatial solutions (right front brain) without becoming emotional about the issue. It's as if emotion is in a little room of its own and a man's smaller corpus callosum means that emotion is less likely to operate simultaneously with other functions.

For women, emotion operates on a more widely spread area in both hemispheres and thus can operate at the same time as other brain functions. A woman can become emotional while discussing an emotional issue, while a man is less likely to do the same, or he will simply refuse to discuss the issue. This way, he can avoid becoming emotional or appear not to be in control. Overall, women's emotions can switch on simultaneously with most other brain functions meaning that she can cry while changing a flat tyre, whereas a man sees tyre-changing as a test of his problem-solving abilities, and will remain completely dry-eyed even when he discovers, by the side of a deserted road, at midnight, in the pouring rain, that the spare is flat and he took the jack from the boot of the car last week.

An emotional man can lash

out like a reptile; an emotional

woman prefers to 'talk about it'.

Ruben Gur, professor of neuro-psychology at the University of Pennsylvania, pioneered similar research and concluded that men's brains, being highly compartmentalised, deal with emotions on a more basic animal level, similar to an attacking crocodile, whereas a woman will 'sit down and talk about it'. When a woman is talking with emotion, she uses expressive facial signals, body language and a range of speech patterns. A man who switches on his emotions is more likely to go into a reptilian mode and lash out vocally or become aggressive.

Women Value Relationships, Men Value Work

Modern society is a mere blip on the screen of human evolution. Hundreds of thousands of years of living in traditional roles has left modern men and women with brain circuitry that causes most of our relationship problems and misunderstandings. Men have always defined themselves by their work and accomplishments and women define their own self-worth by the quality of their relationships. A man is a lunch-chaser and problem solver – this had to be his priority for survival. A woman is a nest-defender – her role was to ensure survival of the next generation. All the studies conducted on male and female values in the 1990s continued to show that 70%–80% of men everywhere still say that the most important part of their lives is their work, and 70%–80% of women say the most important priority is their families. As a consequence,

If a woman is unhappy in her relationships, she can't concentrate on her work. If a man is unhappy at work he can't focus on his relationships.

Under stress or pressure, a woman sees spending time talking with her man as a reward, but a man sees it as an interference in his problem-solving process. She wants to talk and cuddle, and he wants to watch the football. To a woman, he seems uncaring and disinterested and a man sees her as annoying or pedantic. These perceptions are the reflections of the different organisation and priorities of their brains. This is why a woman always says that the relationship seems more important to her that it does to him –

147

it is. Understanding this difference will take the pressure off you and your partner, and you will not judge each other's behaviour harshly.

Why Men 'Do Things'

A man's brain is organised to evaluate and understand objects, their relationship to other objects, spatial relevance, how it all works and solutions to problems. His brain is programmed for a 'how-do-I-fix-it?' response to life. Men use this 'fix it' criterion in their approach to almost everything they do. One woman told us that she wanted her husband to show a more loving attitude towards her – so he mowed the lawn. He saw this as an expression of his love. When she said she still wasn't happy, he painted the kitchen. And when this didn't work, he offered to take her to the football. When a woman is upset she will talk emotionally to her friends, but an upset man will rebuild a motor or fix a leaking tap.

To prove his love for her, he climbed the highest mountain, swam the deepest ocean, and crossed the widest desert. But she left him – he was never home.

While women fantasise about love and romance, men fantasise about fast cars, bigger computers, boats and motorcycles. All these are things they can use and all are related to spatial ability and 'doing something'.

Why Men and Women Leave Each Other

A man's biological urge is to provide for a woman and her appreciation of his efforts confirms his success. If she is happy, he feels fulfilled. If she is not happy he feels that he is a failure because he believes he can't provide enough. Men constantly say to their friends, 'I can never make her happy,' and this can be sufficient motivation for a man to leave a relationship for another woman who seems happy with what he can provide.

A woman leaves a man not because

she is unhappy with what he can

provide, but because she is

emotionally unfulfilled.

She wants love, romance and conversation. He needs to be told by a woman that he is successful at what he does and what he can provide is fine. But a man needs to be romantic and, most of all, listen when a woman talks, without offering solutions.

Why Men Hate to Be Wrong

To understand why men hate to be wrong, it's important to understand the history of where this attitude came from. Picture this scene. The cave family is crouched around a fire. The man is sitting at the cave entrance gazing out, surveying the landscape and scanning the horizon for signs of movement. The woman and children have not eaten for days and he knows that he must hunt at the first break in the weather and not return until he has found food. This is his role and his family are depending on him. They're hungry but confident he can succeed as he has always done. His stomach is churning and he is fearful. Will he be successful again? Will his family starve? Will other males kill him because he is weak from hunger? He just sits there with a blank expressionless face – watching. He must not show any signs of fear to his family as they would become disheartened. He must be strong.

> *In being wrong, a man considers*
>
> *himself a failure because he has*
>
> *not been able to do his job properly.*

A million years of not wanting to be seen as a failure seems to be wired into the brains of modern men. Most women do not know that if a man is driving in the car alone, he'd probably stop and ask directions. But to do it when she is in the car makes him feel like he is a failure because he couldn't get her there.

When a woman says, 'Let's ask directions', a man hears: 'You're incompetent, you can't navigate'. If she says, 'The kitchen tap is leaking, let's call a plumber', he hears, 'You're useless, I'll get another man to do it!' This is also the reason men have difficulty saying, 'I'm sorry'. They see it as admitting they are wrong, and to be wrong is to fail.

To deal with this problem, a woman needs to make sure that she doesn't make a man feel wrong when she discusses problems with him. Even giving a man a self-help book for his birthday is often interpreted by him as, 'You're not good enough.'

> *Men hate criticism – that's why*
>
> *they like to marry virgins.*

A man needs to understand that a woman's objective is not to make him wrong; it's to help him and he should not take things personally. A woman wants to improve the man she loves but he interprets this as meaning that he is not good enough. A man won't admit mistakes because he thinks she won't love him. But the reality is, a woman loves a man more when he will admit mistakes.

Why Men Hide Their Emotions

Modern men still carry the ancient legacy of being brave and showing no weaknesses. Women everywhere ask, 'Why does he always have to be so strong? Why can't he just show me how he feels?' 'When he's angry or upset he bottles it up and becomes cut-off or distant.' 'It's like pulling teeth to get him to discuss his problems.'

By nature, a man is suspicious, competitive, controlled, defensive and a loner who hides his emotional state to stay in control. For men, becoming emotional is seen as being out of control. Social conditioning reinforces these behaviours in men by teaching them to 'act like a man', 'put on a brave face' and 'boys don't cry'.

As a nest-defender, a woman's brain is pre-wired to be open, trusting, co-operative, show vulnerability, reveal emotions and know it's not necessary to stay in control all the time. This is why, when a man and woman encounter problems together, each is confused about the other's reaction.

Why Men Hang Out with the Boys

For our caveman, the big food prizes were much larger and stronger than him, so he organised himself into co-operative groups with others to form a hunting pack. His superior brain allowed him to create the ancient equivalent of football plays for hunting and he used a system of body language signals to allow his hunting strategies to be deployed.

These hunting packs consisted almost entirely of males doing 'men's work', that is, throwing their spears at lunch while the women, who were usually pregnant, did 'women's work' in tending to children, collecting fruits, homemaking and defending the nest. The urge for men to pack-hunt took millions of years to instil into the male brain and no amount of training will remove it overnight. And so modern men meet in hunting packs at pubs and clubs to exchange jokes and tell stories about their hunting activities and when they go home, most still like to sit and gaze into the fire.

Why Men Hate Advice

A man needs to feel that he is capable of solving his own problems and sees discussing them with others as imposing a burden on that person. He won't even bother his best friend with a problem unless he thinks the friend may have a better solution.

Don't offer a man advice unless he asks for it. Tell him you have confidence in his ability to work things out.

When a woman tries to get a man to talk about his feelings or problems, he resists because he sees it as criticism, or feels that she must think he is incompetent and she has a better solution for him. In reality, her objective is to help him feel better and, for a woman, offering advice builds trust in a relationship and is not seen as a sign of weakness.

Why Men Offer Solutions

Men have logical, problem-solving minds. When a man enters a room in a conference centre or restaurant for the first time, he looks around and sees things that need fixing, pictures that need straightening and better ways of laying out the room. His brain is a problem-solving machine that never takes a holiday. Even if he was on his death bed in hospital he'd be thinking of better ways to arrange the ward to take advantage of the natural light and country views.

Talking about her problems is how

a woman gets relief from stress.

But she wants to be heard, not fixed.

When a woman talks about her problems, a man continually interrupts her and offers solutions. He can't help himself because his brain is programmed to do this. He thinks she will feel much better when she has a solution. She only wants to talk and ignores his solutions. This makes him feel incompetent and a failure or that she is probably blaming him for her problems. Women don't want solutions, they just want to talk about things and for someone to listen.

Why Stressed Women Talk

Under stress or pressure, a man's main brain functions of spatial ability and logic are activated. A woman's speech function is activated and she starts talking, often non-stop. If she's stressed, she talks, talks and talks to anyone who will listen. She can talk about her problems to her friends for hours, giving a thorough report of details and then they all give the problem another post-mortem. She talks about present problems, past problems, possible problems and problems that have no solutions. When she talks, no solutions are sought as she receives comfort and relief from the process of talking. Her talk is unstructured and several subjects can be discussed at any one time with no conclusions being reached.

For a woman, sharing problems with her friends is a sign of trust and friendship.

For a man, listening to her talk about problems is hard work because he feels he is expected to solve each problem she brings up as she talks aloud. He doesn't just want to talk about it, he wants to *do* something about it! He is likely to interrupt with, 'What's the point here?' The point is that there doesn't *need* to be a point. The most valuable lesson a man can learn is to listen using listening sounds and gestures, and not to offer solutions. To a man, however, this is an alien concept because he only talks when he has a solution to offer.

When you're dealing with an upset woman, don't offer solutions or invalidate her feelings – just show her you're listening.

When a woman refuses to accept his solutions, his next strategy is to try to minimise the problems by telling her, 'It doesn't really matter', 'You're overreacting', 'Forget about it', and 'It's not a big deal'. This infuriates a woman who begins to feel he doesn't care about her because he won't listen.

Why Stressed Men Won't Talk

A woman talks outside her head, that is, you can hear her, whereas a man talks inside his head. He doesn't have strong brain areas for speech so this suits his mindset. When he has a problem he talks to himself while she talks to other people.

This is why, when under the pressure of problems or stress, a man will clam up and stop talking. He uses his right brain to try to solve his problems or find solutions and he stops using his left brain to listen or speak. His brain can only do 'one thing at a time'. He can't solve problems and listen or talk simultaneously. This silence is often distressing and frightening for a woman. A women says to her husband, son and brother, 'Come on, you've got to talk about it! You'll feel better!' She says this because this is what works for her. But he just wants to be left alone to firegaze until he comes up with some solutions and answers. He doesn't want to talk to anyone about it, especially a therapist, because he sees that as a major sign of weakness.

The famous Rodin sculpture *'The Thinker'* symbolises a man thinking about his problems. He wants to sit on his rock and think about solutions and needs to be alone to do it. The key word here is *alone* – no-one is ever allowed to go up on the rock with him, not even his best friends. In fact, his male friends would not even contemplate going up there. A women feels the urge to climb up there with him to give comfort and she gets a rude shock when he pushes her off!

Men climb on to their rock to solve problems. Women who follow them get kicked off.

If Rodin created a sculpture to personify a woman, it would probably be called *'The Talker'*. Women need to understand that when a man is on his rock they need to leave him there and let him think. Many women feel that his silence means he doesn't love her or that he's angry with her. This is because if a woman wasn't talking, she'd be angry or upset. But if she leaves him on his rock with a cup of tea and a biscuit and doesn't press him to talk, he'll be fine. When he finally solves his problem, he'll come down off his rock and feel happy and begin to talk again.

Using Spatials to Solve Problems

The different ways men 'sit on their rock' include reading a newspaper or magazine, playing squash, fishing, tennis, golf, fixing something or watching television. A man who is under pressure is likely to invite another man to play golf and when they play, there will be limited conversation. The man with the problem goes into his right brain to use his spatial skills to play golf and can use this area to simultaneously work out solutions for his problem. It seems that stimulating his spatial area speeds up the problem-solving process.

Why Men Flick the TV Channels

A man flicking the channels with the remote control is one of women's pet hates. He sits there like a zombie just flicking, not paying attention to any particular programme. When a man does this, he is mentally sitting on his rock and often doesn't even see what's happening on each station. He just searches for the bottom line in each story. By channel-flicking he can forget about his problems and look for solutions to other people's. Women don't flick channels – they watch a programme and search for the storyline, the feelings and relationships of those involved in the story. Newspaper addiction serves the same purpose for men. Women need to understand that when men do these things they can't hear or remember much, so it is difficult to try to talk with them. Instead, make an appointment and give him an agenda. Remember, his forefathers spent over a million years sitting expressionless on a rock surveying the horizon, so this comes naturally to him and he is comfortable doing it.

How to Get Boys to Talk

Mothers everywhere lament the fact their sons won't talk to them. Their daughters come home from school and pour their hearts out about everything, whether it's significant or not. Males are programmed to 'do things' and so this is the key to getting boys to talk. A mother who wants to communicate more with her son should get involved in an activity with him – painting, gym, computer games – and then talk during the activity.

Boys don't like too much eye

contact, but mothers love it.

This way he can avoid too much eye contact, even though the conversation may be disjointed because he has to stop the activity from time to time to respond to a question. It's difficult for him to do two things at once, but the main objective here is to get him to talk. The same strategy also works with a man but don't talk to him at a critical time – like while he's screwing in a lightbulb!

When They're Both Stressed

Uptight men drink alcohol and invade another country. Uptight women eat chocolate and invade shopping centres. Under pressure, women talk without thinking and men act without thinking. That's why 90% of people in jails are men and 90% of people who see therapists are women. When men and women are both under pressure it can be an emotional minefield as each tries to cope. Men stop talking and women become worried about it. Women start talking and men can't handle it. To help him feel better she tries to encourage him to talk about the problem, which is the worst thing she can do. He tells her to leave him alone and retreats to another location.

Men need to understand that when a woman is stressed, she wants to talk, and all he needs to do is listen, not offer solutions.

Because she's also under pressure, she wants to talk about her problems, which frustrates him even more. When he retreats to his rock she feels rejected and unloved and calls her mother, sister or friends.

The Complete Shut-Out

This is one of the least understood stress differences between men and women. A man will completely shut everyone out when he is under extreme stress or needs to find a solution to a serious problem. A man totally disconnects the part of his brain that controls emotion, goes into problem-solving mode and stops talking. When a man uses the complete shut-out, it can be terrifying for a woman because she only does this when she has been hurt, lied to or abused. A woman assumes that this must also be the case with a man – she must have hurt him and he doesn't love her anymore. She tries to encourage him to talk but he refuses, thinking she doesn't have faith is his ability to solve his problems. When a woman feels hurt, she shuts off and a man thinks she needs space and so he goes to the pub with his friends or cleans the carburettor in his car. If a man completely shuts off, let him do it, he'll be fine. If a woman shuts off, there's trouble brewing and it's time for deep discussion.

How Men Alienate Women

If a man suspects that a woman is stressed or has a problem, he does what men do to other men – he walks away and gives her some space to solve her problems. He says, 'Is everything OK honey?', she replies, 'Yes, fine...' which is indirect talk for, 'If you love me you'll ask me about it'. But he says, 'That's good', and goes off to work on his computer. She thinks, 'He's uncaring and heartless' and calls her girlfriends. They talk about how she feels and how insensitive her man is.

In the old days, men never had to face the problems that modern men face. To show his love for his wife and family a man did what men have always done – he went to work and 'brought home the bacon'. This is the way it has been for thousands of years and it comes naturally to most men. In most countries the workforce now averages around 50% females so many men are no longer expected to provide completely for their families: A man is expected to communicate: a skill that does not come naturally to him. But the good news is, these skills can be learned.

Why Men Can't Handle Women Being Emotional

When a woman is upset or emotional she may cry, wave her arms around and constantly talk using emotional adjectives to describe how she feels. She wants to be mothered, taken care of and listened to, but a man interprets her behaviour based on his own priorities and he hears her saying, 'Save me, fix my problems!'

So instead of being reassuring and comforting, he offers advice, asks probing questions or tells her not to be so upset. 'Stop crying!' he says with a terrified look on his face. 'You're over-reacting! Things aren't that bad!' Instead of mothering her, he becomes her father. He saw his father and grandfather behave this way and this is how men have behaved since they climbed out of the trees. For a woman, her display of emotion is a form of communication which she can get over and forget quickly, but a man feels responsible for finding a solution for her and feels like a failure if he can't think of one. This is why, when a woman is emotional, a man gets upset or angry and tells her to stop. Men also get scared when a woman won't stop crying.

The Crying Game

Women cry more than men. Because of the way men evolved they don't cry much, especially in public, and social conditioning reinforces this. When a boy is playing football and suffers a really painful injury he might fall to the ground screaming, but a wild-eyed coach shouts, 'Get up! Don't show the opposition they hurt you! Be a man!'

The sensitive New Age Guy, however, is now expected to cry any time, any place. He is encouraged to cry by therapists, counsellors, magazine articles and at retreats where men hug each other around camp fires, deep in the forest. Modern men are accused of being cold or dysfunctional if they don't 'let it all out' at every opportunity. Because a woman's brain can connect emotion to other brain functions it is obvious why she can cry or become emotional under most conditions.

Real men do cry, but only when the emotion segment of the brain is engaged.

Real men do cry but only when they are tapping the emotion segment of the brain, and men will rarely let this happen in public. So be suspicious of the man who does it regularly in public. Women have superior sensory abilities compared to men. They receive more detailed information than men and are more able to express emotionally and verbally how they feel. A woman may cry at being insulted because an insult is usually emotionally charged but a man may not even be aware that he has been insulted. It literally doesn't mean much to him.

Eating Out

Women see eating out as a way to build and nurture a relationship, discuss problems or support a friend. Men see it as a logical approach to food – no cooking, shopping or cleaning up. When eating out, women call everyone by their first names because this builds relationships, but men will avoid any intimacy with other men. If Barbara, Robyn, Lisa and Fiona go to lunch they will call each other Barbara, Robyn, Lisa and Fiona. But if Ray, Allan, Mike and Bill go out for a drink, they refer to each other as Dickhead, Wanker, Numbskull and Useless. These names avoid any hint of intimacy.

When the bill arrives, the women calculate who had what. The men all throw $100 on the table indicating they want to pay so they can grab the spotlight, each pretending that they really don't want the change.

Shopping: Her Joy, His Terror

For women, shopping is like talking – it does not need to have a specific point or objective and can take place in an unstructured way over several hours. It doesn't need a definite outcome. Women find shopping rejuvenating and relaxing, whether or not they buy anything. This type of shopping gives a man a brain haemorrhage within 20 minutes. For a man to feel energised he needs an objective, a target to hit and a timetable. After all, he's a lunch-chaser – that's his job. He wants to make a quick kill and take it home.

Most men get a brain haemorrhage

after 20 minutes of shopping.

Men become anxious and frustrated in a dress shop when a woman tries on outfit after outfit, asks for his opinion and then buys nothing. Women love testing a wide range of clothes because it fits the pattern of their brain – a range of emotions and feelings and each different outfit to reflect that mood. A man's clothing reflects the male brainset – predictable, conservative and bottom-line oriented. That's why it's easy to spot a man who gets a woman to buy his clothes for him. A man who is a good dresser usually has a woman choosing his clothes or he's gay. One in eight men are colour blind to either blue, red or green and most have little ability to match patterns and designs. That's why it's easy to spot a single man.

To motivate a man to go shopping, give him clear criteria – colours, sizes, brands, styles – and tell him where you will shop and for how long. With clear objectives (even if you've invented them), you'll be amazed at a man's shopping enthusiasm.

How to Give a Woman a Sincere Compliment

When a woman tries on a new dress and asks a man, 'How does it look?', she'll probably receive a simple response like 'good' or 'fine' which does not score any points. To score good points a man needs to respond the same way a woman would, by *giving details*.

Some men cringe at the thought
of responding in detail, but if
you are prepared to try it, you will
score big points with most women.

For example, if he said, 'Wow! Great choice! Turn around, let me see the back. That colour really suits you! The cut flatters your figure. Those earrings match your outfit perfectly, you look wonderful,' most women would be extremely impressed.

CHAPTER 7
OUR CHEMICAL COCKTAIL

'Let me get this straight, Mrs Goodwin. You say you're suffering PMT, you warned your husband that unless he stopped flicking channels on the remote control you'd blow his brains out ... How did he respond?'

Peter asks Paula to go to dinner. They have a great time. In fact, they get on so well they decide to go steady and exchange friendship rings. A year later they're driving home from the movies and Paula asks Peter what he would like to do to celebrate their first anniversary. Peter says, 'We could order in some pizza and then watch the golf on TV!' Paula becomes silent. Peter suspects there's a problem and says, 'Well, if you don't want pizza we can order Chinese.' Paula replies, 'Fine!' and remains quiet.

Peter is thinking, 'A year already! So it was January when we started going out and that's when I bought this car so it's due for its 12 months' service. That mechanic said he'd fix that flicking oil light on the dashboard, and that gearbox still isn't working properly!'

Meanwhile, Paula is thinking, 'He doesn't think much of our relationship if he wants to watch TV and eat pizza on our special anniversary. The next thing he'll want is his friends over as well. I'd like a candlelight dinner, some dancing and to talk about our future. This relationship obviously isn't as important to him as it is to me. Maybe he's been feeling confined by it. I want a stronger commitment from him but he's feeling threatened. Come to think of it, sometimes I wish I had a little more space myself so that I could spend more time with my friends. In fact, I need more time to think about where this relationship is heading. I mean, where *are* we going? Are we just going to keep dating or are we going to get married? Have kids? Or what? Am I ready for this level of commitment? Do I really want to be with him for the rest of my life?'

Peter notices the oil light flickering again, frowns and

thinks, 'Those idiots at the garage promised they'd fixed that light and now the car's almost out of warranty!'

Paula is watching him and starts on another train of thought. 'He's frowning ... he's not happy ... I bet he thinks I'm too fat and I should improve the way I dress. I know I should wear less make-up and exercise more. He always talks about how fit my friend Carrie is and that I should go to the gym with her. I've talked to my girlfriends about this and they think that Peter should love me the way I am and not try and change me. Maybe they're right!'

Peter's thoughts, however, are miles away. 'I'm gonna tell those mechanics where to get off! I'll tell them to go to ...'

Paula, still looking at Peter's face, thinks, 'He's really upset now. I can see it on his face and I can feel his tension. Maybe I'm reading him wrong ... maybe he wants more of a commitment from me and he's sensed that I'm feeling a little unsure about how I feel ...Yes, that's it! That's why he's not talking to me ... he doesn't want to open up to me about his feelings in case I reject him. I can see the hurt in his eyes.'

Peter is thinking, 'They'd better get it right this time! I told them I was having problems and they blamed the manufacturer. They'd better not try and tell me the problem isn't covered under warranty or they'll have a fight on their hands. I paid a fortune for this car so they can just ...'

'Peter?' says Paula.

'What?' snaps Peter, annoyed at having his thoughts disturbed.

'Please don't torture yourself like this ... maybe I'm wrong to be thinking this way ... Oh, I feel so bad ... Maybe I just need some time ... I mean life wasn't meant to be easy ...'

'That's for sure!' Peter grunts.

'You probably think I'm being foolish, don't you?'

'No,' says Peter, confused.

'It's just that … oh, I don't know any more … I'm confused … I need some time to think about this,' she says.

Peter thinks, 'What the hell is she talking about? I'll just say "OK" and she'll be over it tomorrow! It must be that time of the month.'

'Thank you Peter … you don't know how much this means to me,' she says. Looking into his eyes she realises he is a very special person and she will need to think very hard about this relationship.

She tosses and turns all night and next morning calls her friend Carrie to discuss it. They decide to meet for lunch and talk about Peter and the problems. Meanwhile, Peter went home, opened a beer and turned on the TV. He thinks Paula has some sort of problem, probably PMT.

Paula and Carrie meet next day and talk well into the night. A few days later, Peter is talking to Carrie's boyfriend Mark who says, 'So you and Paula are having problems, eh?' Peter is now completely confused. 'I don't know what she's talking about!' laughs Peter ' … but take a look at this oil light and tell me what you think.'

How Hormones Control Us

In the past, it was thought that hormones only affected the body and not the brain. We now know that hormones programme our brains before birth, dictating our thinking and behaviour. Testosterone in teenage boys is 15–20 times higher than in teenage girls and the hormone flow in boys is controlled and regulated by the brain as the body needs it.

At puberty, testosterone surges through an adolescent boy's body, giving him a dramatic spurt of growth and a body ratio of 15% fat and 45% protein. As he turns into an adolescent, his body physically changes to match his biological job description as a lean, mean, lunch-chasing machine. Boys are excellent at sport because their bodies are hormonally constructed for effective breathing and they have excellent oxygen distribution via the red blood cells to allow running, jumping and grappling. Steroids are male hormones that build additional muscle and give athletes extra 'hunting' abilities and an unfair advantage over non-steroid takers.

Female hormones have a different effect on teenage girls. They are not regulated like a boy's hormones but come in huge waves over a 28-day cycle and can cause havoc for many girls and women due to the rise and fall of emotions that go with it. Female hormones change a girl's body into a ratio of 26% fat and 20% protein, much to the frustration of females everywhere. The purpose of the extra fat is to give additional energy for breastfeeding and is insurance against times when food may be scarce. Because female hormones fatten the body, they are used to fatten livestock. Male hormones reduce fat and build muscle so they're unsuitable for animal fattening.

The Chemicals of 'Falling in Love'

You've just met that special person. Your heart is racing, your hands are sweating, you've got butterflies in your stomach and you tingle all over. You go to dinner together and you feel as high as a kite. At the end of the evening, your date kisses you and it makes you melt. For days after, you don't eat but you've never felt better and you've noticed your cold is cured.

Neural evidence shows that the phenomenon of 'falling in love' is a series of chemical reactions taking place in the brain that cause mental and physical reactions. There are an estimated 100 billion neurones that make up the brain's communication network. Candace Pert, author of *Molecules of Emotion* (1999), pioneered the research that discovered neuropeptides, a string of amino acids that float around the body and attach themselves to welcoming receivers. So far, 60 different neuropeptides have been discovered and they trigger emotional reactions in the body when they attach themselves to the receivers. In other words, all our emotions – love, grief, happiness – are all biochemical. When English scientist Francis Crick and his associates won the Nobel Prize in Medicine for deciphering the DNA code that defines genes, he stunned the medical world by saying, 'You, your joys, sorrows, memories, ambitions, your sense of identity, free will and love are no more than the behaviour of a vast assembly of nerve cells.'

The main chemical released to give you the elated physical feelings of being in love is PEA (phenylethylamine) which is related to amphetamines and is found in chocolate. This is one of the chemicals that makes your heart race, hands sweat, pupils dilate and gives you 'butterflies' in the stomach. Adrenalin is also released, speeding up your heart, making you alert and helping you feel great. Along with that are also the endorphins, which build your immune system and cure your cold. When you both kissed, your brains made a rapid chemical analysis of each other's saliva and it made decisions on your genetic compatibility. The woman's brain also made chemical determinations about the state of the man's immune system.

All this positive chemical reaction explains why people in love have been shown to have better health and are much less likely to contract an illness than those who are not. Being in love is usually great for your health.

Hormonal Chemistry

Oestrogen is the female hormone that gives women an overall feeling of contentment and well-being, and plays a major role in a woman's nurturing and nest-defending behaviours. Because of its calming effect, it is also given to aggressive males in prisons to control violent behaviour. Oestrogen also aids memory, which explains why so many women suffer memory problems after menopause when their oestrogen levels drop. Those who are on Hormone Replacement Therapy (HRT) have better memory retention.

Experiments in June 2000 by Dr Agnes Lacreuse of Emory University in Atlanta showed that as the ratio of testosterone to oestrogen changes most women will experience an enhancement in spatial memory. This can make it easier for them to remember where car keys, glasses or handbags have been left – or where they parked the car.

Progesterone is the hormone that releases parental and nurturing feelings and its purpose is to encourage a woman to carry out her child-rearing role successfully. Progesterone is released when a woman sees a baby and research shows it is the baby's shape that triggers the release of the hormone. A baby has short, stubby arms and legs, a round, plump torso, oversized head and large eyes, and these shapes are known as 'releasers'. The reaction to this shape is so strong that the hormone is also released when a woman sees these shapes in an object like a stuffed toy. This is why toys such as teddy bears and baby animals sell so well to females and long, gangly-shaped toys don't. A woman or girl will pick up a teddy bear and sigh, 'Ahh ... isn't it beautiful!' and progesterone is released into her bloodstream.

Most men, lacking progesterone hormones, can't understand a woman's over-reaction to a piece of high-priced stuffed merchandise. This could also explain why women who are the mothering type marry short fat men with chubby cheeks.

Baby   Teddy bear   Skinny toy

Look at these three illustrations. Seeing the baby causes the release of progesterone hormone in women and the toy bear has the same effect. There are no releaser shapes in the third example so it will not release progesterone in a woman. The best selling toys have always been plump dolls and baby animals with dilated pupils.

Why Blondes Have High Fertility

Blonde hair is a sign of high oestrogen levels and accounts for men's strong attraction to blondes. It is an indicator of fertility and is the likely explanation of the phrase 'dumb blonde'. Dumb blondes, so the jokes go, have high fertility and low mathematical reasoning. Research has shown that teenage girls whose mothers took male hormones during pregnancy perform better in academic disciplines than other females, and are more likely to get into university. The other side of the coin is that these girls are described as less feminine in nature and are likely to have more body hair.

After a blonde's first baby is born, her hair darkens because her oestrogen level drops. It darkens even more after her second child. The reduction in oestrogen levels is why there are few natural blondes after age 30.

In the Roman era, prostitutes wore blonde wigs as an advertisement for their trade and this gave rise to the phrase, 'Blondes have more fun.'

PMT and Sex Drive

Pre-Menstrual Tension (PMT) is a major problem for modern women and one with which their ancestors never had to deal. Until recently, women tended to be pregnant most of the time, which meant that the average woman only ever had to deal with menstrual-related problems 10 to 20 times in a lifetime, versus 13 times a year for modern women. If she has the average of 2.4 children, this adds up to 350–400 times a modern woman can suffer PMT symptoms in her child-bearing years between ages 12 to 50, and close to 500 times for a woman without children.

Until the introduction of the contraceptive pill in the 1950s, no-one noticed that women had emotional highs and lows. For the first 21 days after menstruation, oestrogen hormones create a feeling of well-being and give generally happy feelings and a positive attitude to most premenopausal women. Sex drive gradually increases so that she is most capable of conceiving at a specific point, about midway through the cycle. This is also the time when her testosterone level is the highest.

Nature is clever. It has a timetable for most female animals that makes them randiest at the most likely time for conception. This is easily observable in many female animals. With horses for example, the female on heat teases and excites the male but won't let him mount until the exact second when the egg is in the right position for fertilisation. Female humans are unaware that a similar timetable and reactions apply to them too.

This is how a woman may inexplicably find herself in bed with a man she's just met at a party and the next day is at a total loss to understand how or why it happened. 'I don't know what happened,' said one woman. 'I met him at a party and, before I knew it, we were in bed together! I've never done that before!' Like other female animals, she happened to meet this man at the right time of the month and at the precise moment for the highest chance of conception. His genetic make-up, the state of his immune system and other male characteristics were decoded sub-consciously by the woman's brain. If they passed a certain rating level of acceptability for being a potential father, nature took control. Women who have experienced this event don't know how to explain it, and many describe it as 'fate' or 'a strange magnetic attraction', instead of under-standing that their hormones simply took control. As a result of these moments, many women get stuck in life with men who are unsuitable partners. Most men would give anything to know when a woman is at her hormonal peak!

Scottish scientists studied the reactions and preferences of 104 women to digitally altered photos of men. They found that during three weeks of the month women pre-ferred the smoother, more feminised, sensitive looking types who would be more likely to be around over the long haul. When the women were ovulating, however, they favoured the manly-looking men – big jaws, prominent eye-brows and larger bodies – the stuff that screams virility. They also observed that many ovulating women wore shorter skirts in public. The scientists concluded that when it comes to settling down, women want a male who is the best parental investment. But when the biological bells are ringing, they want Tarzan's genes.

Woman's Chemical Gloom

Between 21–28 days after menstruation, female hormones dramatically drop, creating severe withdrawal symptoms commonly known as PMT. For many women, this causes feelings of doom, gloom, depression, and even suicidal tendencies. One in 25 women suffer so severely from their hormones being out of balance, she can undergo personality changes.

Several studies have found that most female crime such as assault and shoplifting occurs during the 21–28 days pre-menstrual period. It has been found in women's prisons that at least 50% of female murders or assaults are committed by women suffering PMT. Women's visits to psychiatrists, counsellors and astrologers increase dramatically during this phase and many women feel that they are 'losing control' or 'going crazy'. There are well documented studies showing that women suffering PMT are four to five times more likely to be involved in a car accident when they are behind the wheel.

Female hormones have long been used as a way of pacifying habitually aggressive people. In some countries, PMT is a factor accepted by judges when considering sentencing for women charged with violent crimes.

When a woman reaches menopause, usually in her 40s or early 50s, she goes through a variety of psychological, emotional and hormonal changes. These vary from woman to woman.

Menopause in men, however, is a uniformly predictable event – he buys aviator sunglasses, leather driving gloves, gets a hair transplant, goes shopping for a motorcycle or sports car, and wears funny clothes.

Testosterone: Bonus or Curse?

Male hormones, particularly testosterone, are the aggression hormones that cause men to hunt and kill prey. Testosterone is largely responsible for human survival, as it drove men to catch food and fight off attackers. It is also the hormone that makes men's beards grow, causes baldness, deepens voices and improves spatial ability. Bass baritones have been shown to enjoy more than double the number of ejaculations in a week than tenors, and most people given a course of testosterone have less difficulty reading maps and street directories. Interestingly, left-handedness and asthma have also been linked to testosterone and it is now known that men who smoke or drink excessively have reduced levels in their blood.

The downside of testosterone for modern males is that unless it is allowed to vent itself in a physical outlet, it may create aggression and can cause anti-social problems. As testosterone surges through their bodies, boys aged between 12 and 17 enter the highest male crime bracket. Give a passive man testosterone and it will fire him up and he'll become more assertive and self-reliant. The same dosage given to a woman can also raise her aggression level, but will not have the same degree of chemical effect as for a man. His brain is pre-wired to react to testosterone while a woman's is not. The reason for this is still uncertain, but it is obviously related to spatial ability.

Women should watch out for left-handed, bald, bearded accountants with baritone voices who read maps and sneeze at the same time.

As men reach their 50s and 60s, testosterone decreases and they become less aggressive and more nurturing. For women, the reverse happens. After menopause, oestrogen levels decrease giving them a bigger ratio of testosterone to oestrogen. This is why women aged 45–50 suddenly become more assertive and more self-reliant. The downside is that these women are more likely to grow facial hair and suffer stress and strokes.

The Case of the Flying Crockery

Author Barbara Pease was unaware that the new contraceptive pill she had been given contained a high level of testosterone. Her husband, Allan, quickly learned the valuable art of ducking from flying plates and other airborne objects during Barbara's PMT phase, and rediscovered his childhood facility for the short-distance sprint. Interestingly, her parallel parking abilities – or lack thereof – no longer started arguments. They improved dramatically on this pill.

Blood tests eventually revealed Barbara's testosterone excess and she changed to a pill without it. Within a month, her mood swings had virtually ceased, but now Allan felt he was living with a librarian studying to be a nun. Another change of pill raised her testosterone level back up to a happy medium, much safer both for their marriage, and the household crockery.

Why Men Are Aggressive

Testosterone is the hormone of success, achievement and competitiveness and in the wrong hands (or testicles) makes men and male animals potentially dangerous. Most parents are aware of the almost insatiable desire that young boys have to watch violent movies and how their sons can accurately recall and describe aggressive scenes in detail. Girls are generally uninterested in these types of movies. A study at the University of Sydney showed that when confronted with a potentially aggressive conflict such as a schoolyard fight, 74% of boys used verbal or physical aggression to solve the problem whereas 78% of girls tried to walk away or negotiate the situation. Ninety-two per cent of horn tooting at traffic lights is done by men, while they also carry out 96% of burglaries and 88% of murders. Practically all sexual deviants are male, and tests on deviant women show high male hormone levels.

Ninety percent of the
people in prison are men.

Male aggression is mainly responsible for men's dominance of our species. We don't teach aggression to boys, we try to condition them away from it. Aggression is one male trait that cannot be explained by social conditioning.

Studies with sportsmen show their testosterone level is significantly higher at the end of an event than before it, demonstrating neatly how competition can build levels of aggression. New Zealand sports teams are often seen performing the Maori war dance, the *haka*, immediately before the start of play. This serves two purposes: to strike fear into their opponents and to raise the testosterone levels of the performers. Cheerleaders are used in many sports worldwide for exactly the same reason, to raise the testosterone levels of players and supporters. Studies confirm that higher levels of crowd violence occur in matches where cheerleaders are used.

Why Men Work So Hard

Professor James Dabbs of Georgia State University took saliva samples from men ranging from business leaders and politicians to sportsmen, priests and convicts. He found the top performers in each field had higher testosterone levels than the poorer performers, and the lowest counts were recorded by clergymen, indicating less dominant and less sexually active lives. He also found that high female achievers, such as lawyers and sales people, had higher testosterone levels than the average woman. In addition, he reported that not only does testosterone lead to high levels of achievement, but achievement causes more testosterone to be produced.

We have observed animal behaviour from Africa to the jungles of Borneo and witnessed first-hand what scientists have spent years in researching – that the male animals with the highest testosterone levels usually rule the roost. The testosterone in some animals, such as spotted hyenas, is so high that they are born with a full set of teeth and are so aggressive that the young often eat each other.

Creatures with the highest testosterone

levels rule the animal kingdom.

The top dogs, cats, horses, goats, and monkeys are those that record the highest level of male hormone. Put two women together and the one with more testosterone will dominate the interaction. Working women have higher levels than women who stay at home, and daughters of working women have higher levels than daughters of non-working women. Among 700 male prison inmates in a 1995 study, those with the highest testosterone levels were most likely to be in trouble with the authorities or engage in unprovoked violence. A 1998 study found that trial lawyers, with their life conflict and argument, had higher levels than other lawyers. High testosterone males have dominated the human race throughout history and it is a reasonable assumption that outstanding women leaders in history like Boadicea, Margaret Thatcher, Joan of Arc and Golda Meir received additional male hormone at the six to eight week foetal stage.

There is a serious downside, however, to constant levels of unburned testosterone. A chilling example recently came from America where 118 Law students were given the Minnesota Multiphasic Personality Assessment and their lives were tracked and monitored for 30 years. Those with the highest hostility and aggression levels were four times more likely to have died during the period. As society becomes less physical and more cerebral and women replace men in many industries, we will have to find new ways to channel male testosterone. There is a growing focus on muscular male physique in popular culture, a boom in crass men's magazines and an explosion in violent computer games. This is known as cultural displacement and this happens when the power of testosterone is ignored or attacked, so it re-emerges in cruder, less social forms. These are good reasons for young boys to be encouraged to make a life habit of being physically active on a regular basis.

Testosterone and Spatial Ability

You may have already reached the conclusion that because spatial skill is one of the strongest male attributes, it is linked to testosterone. In Chapter 3 we saw how testosterone is mainly responsible for configuring the brain of the genetic male foetus (XY) and installing the 'software' related to the spatial abilities required for hunting and chasing. Consequently, the more testosterone the body produces, the more male-orientated the brain's behaviour will be. Male rats which are injected with additional male hormone find their way out of a maze quicker than normal male rats. Female rats also improve their navigational performance, but not as dramatically as the males. The aggression level of both sexes increases.

In the Brain-Wiring Test, high testosterone males score between -50 and +50 and usually have less difficulty with map-reading, orienteering, playing video games or hitting a target. They have fast-growing beards, love 'hunting' sports like football, billiards and motor racing and are good reverse parkers. Testosterone is also the hormone that aids single-mindedness and helps avoid fatigue. Studies show that volunteers injected with testosterone show greater endurance in physical activities such as walking and long-distance running, and can concentrate for longer periods of time. Not surprisingly, lesbians also have many of these attributes. Susan Resnick of the Institute of Ageing in the US reported in her findings that girls who received abnormal amounts of male hormone in the womb also had far superior spatial skills compared to their sisters who did not receive the hormone.

Why Women Hate Reverse Parking

While testosterone will improve spatial ability, the female hormone, oestrogen, suppresses it. Women have dramatically less testosterone than men and, as a result, the more feminine the brain, the less the spatial ability. This is why very feminine women are not great reverse parkers or map readers. There is a rare condition known as Turner's Syndrome where a genetic female (XX) is missing one of the X chromosomes and she is known as an XO girl. These girls are super-feminine in all their behaviours and have little or no directional or spatial ability. Never lend your car keys to an XO woman.

Chinese men test significantly lower than Caucasian men in testosterone levels and this is evidenced by their lack of facial hair and low incidence of baldness. Chinese societies report comparatively low numbers of men being charged with violent or aggressive crimes, compared to Caucasian or black men. Rape is less common than among Caucasian men, probably because of lower testosterone levels. This also explains why Asian men generally tested lower on their ability to reverse park.

Mathematics and Hormones

Boys use their right front brain to solve mathematical problems. The spatial area for girls is located on both sides of the brain and tests show that many females use the left front verbal side of the brain to attempt to solve mathematical problems. This is the likely explanation for so many women counting aloud. It also goes a long way to explaining why girls are generally better than boys at basic calculus and their co-operation and commitment to study often gives them the edge over boys in arithmetic or mathematical exams.

Brain development in girls occurs much earlier than in boys, which partially explains why they do better earlier. But after puberty boys catch up and excel in mathematical reasoning as testosterone boosts their spatial ability. Tests of mathematical ability were carried out by Johns Hopkins University in Boston on gifted children aged between 11 and 13. They discovered that the more difficult the tests became, the more the boys' ability exceeded that of the girls. At the easier levels, gifted boys beat gifted girls on a ratio of 2:1; in the middle levels the ratio increased to 4:1; and at the highest degree of difficulty it reached 13:1.

In 1998, Canadian brain research authority Dr Doreen Kimura found that if you double or triple the amount of testosterone in a male, it does not necessarily double or triple his mathematical reasoning skills. This shows that there is probably an optimum level for testosterone effectiveness somewhere in the low to mid-range levels. In other words, King Kong will not necessarily show better mathematical reasoning ability than a man with a slow growing beard. Interestingly, testosterone does improve women's mathematical reasoning more dramatically than it does for men. A woman with a moustache is therefore much more likely to make a better engineer than one who looks like a Barbie doll. Men score higher in map-reading ability in the autumn when their testosterone is at its highest levels.

Girls suffering PMT get lower scores in mathematical exams.

The education system favours boys and disadvantages girls in mathematical exams because studies show that girls suffering PMT have testosterone levels that are significantly lower during this phase. One study showed that girls with PMT scored 14% lower in mathematical exams when they had PMT than girls who weren't suffering PMT. A fairer system would be to arrange exams to take place at a time that is biologically more suitable for girls. Boys can take the tests at any time.

Modern Man's Hunting

Sport is the modern replacement for hunting. Most sporting activities began after the year 1800; prior to that, most of the world's population still hunted animals for food or recreation. The Industrial Revolution of the late 1700s and advanced farming techniques meant that it was no longer necessary to chase and catch food. Thousands of years of men being programmed to hunt suddenly came to a stop and had nowhere to go.

Sport became the answer. More than 90% of modern sports were created between 1800 and 1900 and a few new ones appeared during the 20th Century. Most sports involve running, chasing and hitting targets and allow high testosterone individuals to burn up excess hormones. Research shows that boys who are physically active are the least likely to be involved in crime or aggression, and that young men with criminal records showed the least involvement in sports. Simply, if it's not burnt up on a playing field, it can show up in anti-social ways. On motorways and freeways, road-rage has been almost entirely a male offence. Men compete with each other on the road – women just happen to be there at the time.

Before enrolling in a sports club, examine the objectives, values, role-models and leaders of the club. If they're in it 'for the game' and the game is all-important, then these people are still slaves to their biology – so join a fishing club. There are many clubs like yoga or martial arts that still teach the principles for effective living such as health, relaxation and sound life values. Avoid any clubs that emphasise the financial gains members might make.

Why Men Have Pot Bellies and Women Have Large Rears

Nature distributes excess fat tissue as far from the body's vital organs as possible so as to not impede their effective operation. Usually there is little or no fat around the brain, heart and genitals. Women have additional vital organs – ovaries. Consequently, women capable of bearing children tend not to accumulate excess fat on the belly. Men, having no ovaries, accumulate this excess fat in what is usually called a 'pot belly' and they also get fat on the back. That's why you rarely see men with fat legs. Women's excess fat is distributed on their thighs, rears and under the upper arms to be used as a source of nourishment in breast-feeding. If men had ovaries, they would have bigger thighs and flat bellies too. If the ovaries are removed in a hysterectomy, nature will redistribute fat to the belly.

CHAPTER 8
BOYS WILL BE BOYS, BUT NOT ALWAYS

'And then one day, after a biology class, Elliot finally saw what his classmates silently thought – his testostorone level was not normal.'

What makes a woman a woman and a man a man? Is being gay really a choice? Why does a lesbian prefer women? How did transsexuals manage to get a foot on both sides of the fence? Are you who you are because you had an aggressive mother, or your father was emotionally cold or detached, or was it that you had a crush on your Third Year teacher? Are you who you are because you're a second-born child, raised in poverty, orphaned, from a broken family, a Leo on the cusp of Scorpio or perhaps re-incarnated from a cat?

In this chapter we will look at what happens when a human foetus receives too much or too little male hormone.

Gays, Lesbians and Transsexuals

Research shows that the basic template for the body and brain of a human foetus is female in its structure. As a result men have some redundant female features such as nipples. Men also have mammary glands which do not function but retain the potential to produce milk. There are thousands of recorded cases of lactation in male prisoners of war where starvation led to a diseased liver failing to break down the hormones essential for breast-feeding.

As we now know, six to eight weeks after conception, a male foetus (XY) receives a massive dose of male hormones called androgens which first forms the testes, and then a second dose to alter the brain from a female format to a male configuration. If the male foetus does not receive enough male hormone at the appropriate time, one of two things may happen. Firstly, a baby boy may be born with a brain structure that is more feminine than masculine, in other words, a boy who will most likely be gay by puberty. Secondly, a genetic boy may be born with a fully functioning female brain and a set of male genitals. This person will be transgender. This is a person who is biologically male but feeling as if he is a female. Sometimes a genetic male is born with a set of both male *and* female genitals. Geneticist Anne Moir in her ground-breaking book *Brainsex* documents the many cases of genetic boys being born looking like girls and being raised as girls, only suddenly to find that they have penis and testicles that 'appear' at puberty.

This genetic oddity was discovered in the Dominican Republic and a study with the parents of these 'girls' shows that their parents typically raised them as girls and encouraged stereotypical behaviours such as feminine dress and playing with dolls. Many of these parents were then shocked to discover that they'd ended up with a fully fledged son at puberty when male hormones took over and their 'daughters' suddenly had a penis and reverted to male appearance and typical male behaviour patterns. This change occurred despite all the social conditioning and social pressures for female behaviour.

The fact that most of these 'girls' successfully lived the rest of their lives as males highlights the point that their social environment and upbringing had a limited impact on their adult lives. Clearly, their biology was the key factor in creating their behavioural patterns.

Homosexuality is Part of History

Among the ancient Greeks, homosexuality was not only permitted, it was highly respected. The slim, boyish, youthful figure was their ideal of beauty, and paintings and statues were erected in its honour. Poems were written about the love that prominent older men had for young men. The Greeks believed that male homosexuality served a noble, higher purpose and it inspired youths to become worthy members of the community. They also found that young gay men proved to be some of their most courageous, successful warriors as they would fight 'side-by-side in love with each other'.

In Roman times, Julius Caesar was described as 'every woman's man and every man's woman.'

When Christianity frowned on same-sex relationships and God reportedly brought his vengeance down on the City of Sodom, homosexuality was banned, disappeared into the closet and wasn't seen in public again until recently.

The Victorian era refused to acknowledge that homosexuality existed and, even if it did, it must be the Devil's work and would be severely punished. As we enter the 21st Century, most older generations still believe that homosexuality is a recent phenomenon and an 'unnatural' act. The reality is that it has been around for as long as male foetuses missed out on their sufficient share of male hormones. Amongst primates, homosexual behaviour is used as a way of bonding members of a group or as a form of showing submission to a superior, as is also the case with cattle, cocks and dogs. Lesbianism gained its name from the Greek island of Lesbos. It has never been looked upon with the same contempt as male homosexuality, probably because it is associated more with intimacy, and not labelled so much a 'perversion'.

Is it Genetic or a Choice?

When *Body Language* author Allan Pease and geneticist Anne Moir appeared together on British television in 1991 for the launch of their books *Brainsex* (Mandarin Books) and *Talk Language* (HarperCollins), Moir revealed the results of her research which highlighted what scientists have known for years – homosexuality is inborn, not a choice.

Not only is homosexuality mostly inborn, but the environment in which we are raised plays a lesser role in our behaviour than was previously thought. Scientists have found that as an adolescent or adult, parents' efforts to suppress homosexual tendencies in their off-spring has practically no effect. And because the impact of male hormone (or lack of it) on the brain is the main culprit, most homosexuals are males.

There is no solid evidence that upbringing affects the likelihood of a child becoming homosexual.

For every lesbian (female body with a masculinised brain) there are about eight to ten gay men. If the gay and lesbian movement was to embrace this research and, if the education system taught these findings, homosexual and transsexual people would not encounter as much prejudice. Most people are more tolerant and accepting of a person who has inborn differences than they are of a person who, in their opinion, makes an unacceptable choice. Take, for example, Thalidomide babies, Parkinson's sufferers, autism or people who have cerebral palsy. The public is more accepting of these people because they are usually born with these conditions, as opposed to homosexuals who supposedly choose their lifestyle.

Can we be critical of a person who is born left-handed or dyslexic? Or with blue eyes and red hair? Or with a female brain in a male body? Most homosexual people believe that their homosexuality is a choice and, like many minority groups, often use public forums to display their 'choice', which generates negative attitudes from many members of the public.

He was a dyslexic, agnostic insomniac.

He'd lie awake all night wondering if

there really was a dog.

Sadly, statistics show that over 30% of teenage suicides are committed by gays and lesbians, and that one out of every three transgenders commits suicide. It seems that the realisation of being stuck in the 'wrong body' for the rest of their lives is too much for them. A study into the upbringing of these homosexual teenagers has shown that most were raised in families or communities that taught hatred and rejection towards homosexuals, or in religions that had tried to save some of the 'victims' with prayer or therapy.

Why People Look to the Father

When a boy turns out to be gay, the father may often be blamed. Family members claim that he criticised the son for not being involved with, or competent at, male pursuits as he grew up. This theory holds that the boy rebelled against the father and became gay to spite him, but there is no scientific evidence to support this view. The likely explanation is that the boy was more interested in female pursuits rather than football, motorcycle racing, cars or boxing matches. This would have been a constant source of annoyance for a father with high expectations of his son's male development. In other words, the son's effeminate tendencies are more likely to have contributed to the father's critical or aggressive attitude than vice versa.

Red hair and freckles has the same

occurrence as homosexuality.

If the public understood that scientific evidence shows that most, if not all homosexuality is inborn, there would be as much interest in a gay rally as there would be in a rally for people with red hair and freckles, a genetic combination that occurs at the same rate as homosexuality. The public would be more accepting of homosexuality and gays and lesbians would not have as many problems with self-esteem, and would be treated with more dignity, and far less rejection and ridicule. Ignorance on both sides keeps both apart.

Can the 'Choice' Be Changed?

Gays and lesbians do not choose their sexual orientation any more than heterosexuals do. Scientists and most human sexuality experts agree that homosexuality is an orientation that is unchangeable. Researchers believe that most homosexual orientation develops in the womb, that homosexual patterns are firmly fixed by around age five and that it is outside the control of the person. For centuries, techniques have been used to suppress homosexual feelings in 'sufferers' which have included breast amputation, castration, drug therapy, uterus removal, frontal lobotomy, psychotherapy, electric shock therapy, prayer meetings, spiritual counselling and exorcism. No therapies have ever succeeded. The best they have been able to achieve is to make some bisexuals confine their sexual activities to members of the opposite sex or force some homosexuals to become celibate through guilt or fear, and to push many others to suicide.

Scientists have shown that

homosexuality is an orientation

that is unalterable. It's not a choice.

There is a greater than 90% chance that you, the reader, are heterosexual. Think about how difficult it would be to feel sexually attracted to someone of your own sex and you will begin to understand how it is virtually impossible to create feelings that do not already exist. If it was a choice, as many proclaim, why would any intelligent person choose a way of life that exposes them to so much hostility, prejudice and discrimination? Hormones are responsible, not human choices.

The Case of Identical Gay Twins

Extensive research has been carried out on identical twins who were separated at birth and raised in different families and environments. Numerous tests have been conducted to reliably establish whether certain human traits are genetic or determined by social conditioning. This type of research shows that many human traits are genetically inherited, including neuroticism, depression, introversion/extroversion levels, dominance, a facility for sport and the age of first sexual activity. Assuming that around five percent of the male population is gay, if you analysed 100 gay identical male twins who had been separated from their twin at birth then you would expect that around five percent of the other twins would also be gay, based on the assumption that homosexuality is a choice. Various research groups who studied this question have all come up with the same answer. That answer has been demonstrated by American researchers Dr Richard Pillard of Boston University and psychologist Michael Bailey of North Western University who studied the sexual orientation of sibling boys raised together. Their conclusions were:

The chance of sibling homosexuality is:
- 22% for non-identical twins
- 10% for non-twin or adopted brothers
- 52% for identical twins who share the same genes

The collective research into the gay identical twins who were separated at birth, reveals that over 50% of the lost twin brothers were also gay. Of these, the researchers generally agreed it was likely that 10%–20% of the twins who claimed to be heterosexual were probably homosexuals who were too deep inside the closet to admit it, or bisexuals who chose to describe themselves as heterosexual. This brings the real percentage of gay twins with identical genetic make-up to between 60%–70%, or two out of three, proving convincingly that most homosexuality is created in the womb. It also confirms that upbringing has little, if any, impact on sexual orientation.

It's in their Genes

Based on the theory that gayness is created in the womb, you would expect that all identical gay twins would also be gay, so why is this not the case with the other 30%–40% of the gay twin brothers? Genes have a property called 'penetrance' which is a measure of the gene's power to become effective, and determines how likely that gene is to be switched on and become a dominant gene. For example, the variety of gene that causes Huntington's disease is 100% penetrant, whereas the gene that causes Type One diabetes is only 30% penetrant. This means that if identical twins each have both the Huntington's gene and the diabetes gene, each has a 100% chance of developing Huntington's disease but only a 30% chance of developing diabetes.

Those carrying the 'gay gene' as it is now called, have a 50%–70% chance of becoming gay and this theory explains why all the identical twins brothers were not gay. It is estimated that about 10% of all males carry the 'gay gene' and about half these males will become gay due to the 50%–70% penetrance factor of the gene. Laboratory experiments with rats and monkeys have proved that this sequence of events also happens in other species. While performing these types of sex-altering experiments on humans is illegal, and considered to be ethically wrong, we are aware that these have been successfully conducted in Russia with the same conclusive results.

The 'Gay Gene'

Dean Hamer of the National Cancer Institute in the USA compared the DNA of 40 pairs of homosexual brothers and discovered that 33 had the same genetic markers in the X928 region of the X chromosome, which has been determined to be the approximate location of the gay gene. He also compared the DNA of 36 pairs of lesbian sisters but no corresponding pattern was found. This study further shows that not only is homosexuality mainly a condition affecting males but it is almost certainly genetic. The likelihood of the gene becoming penetrant appears to be largely dependent on the presence of the testosterone hormone six to eight weeks after conception. In addition, there is a small chance that other factors, including social conditioning, may activate the gene in early life, usually before age five.

Gay Fingerprints and Family Studies

In 1998, Canadian brain research pioneer Dr Doreen Kimura reported that she had conducted a study of the number of ridges between two specific points on a person's fingerprints. She discovered that people with high ridge counts on the left hand are better at 'feminine' tasks.

She found that most men have more ridges on their right hands, but that, on average, women and homosexual men are likely to have more ridges on their left hands.

Fingerprint ridge counts

Another study of gay men by the National Cancer Institute has shown that homosexuality runs in families. Data collected on the genetic family members of 114 gay men shows there is a three times greater than average chance that gay men's brothers, uncles, cousins or parents were also gay. Most of the gay male family members were on the mother's side of the family and fewer were on the father's side. This can only be caused genetically, and it indicates that there is a special gene somewhere on the X chromosome. This chromosome is the only one a mother can provide (she has two Xs), further demonstrating the genetic transferability of male homosexuality.

Experimental Changes

Rats are a favourite for scientific research. They have hormones, genes and a central nervous system like humans, but their brains do not develop in the womb like a human's – they develop *after* birth which allows us to see what's going on. Castrate a male rat and he thinks he's a she and becomes a social, nest-building rat. Give testosterone hormones to a newborn female rat and she thinks she's a he, becomes aggressive and tries to mount other female rats. Some female birds, such as canaries, can't sing but if they are injected at a young age with testosterone, they can sing like a male. This is because testosterone affects the wiring of their brain and therefore their abilities.

To achieve this sex-changing result the brain must be altered when it is in an embryonic state. Similar tests on adult rats, birds and monkeys failed to produce such dramatic results because the brain is 'set' during the embryonic stage. For humans the brain is 'set' six to eight weeks after conception. It means that older rats won't change much and neither will older humans.

During a seminar tour of Russia, we met a professor of brain surgery from a local university who disclosed to us that secret brain-altering experiments had been carried out in Russia on humans for some time and that their results were the same as with the rats – they had changed boys into girls and girls into boys by altering their brains in the womb with male hormone. They created their own gay, lesbian and transsexual people. He also reported that there had been occasions where the foetus was not given enough male hormone or was given the hormones at the wrong time of its development. One result was a baby boy with two sets of genitals – a male set and a female set. This genetic accident also occurs from time to time in nature (as it has done in the Dominican Republic) and explains how a baby is born looking like a girl and then suddenly becomes a boy at adolescence.

This research shows what scientists know but are not willing to discuss – that, by controlling the sex of the brain with hormones, the sexuality of a foetus can be determined before birth with an injection of a needle at the right time. This would, however, and quite understandably so, raise obvious moral, ethical and humane questions.

It's What Happens in the Womb

If, during the early stages of pregnancy, testosterone is suppressed and the foetus is male, the chance of giving birth to a gay boy dramatically increases because female hormones become the hormones used to configure the brain. One German study in the 1970s showed that mothers who suffered severe stress during early pregnancy had six times the chance of giving birth to a gay son. Research by Professor Lee Ellis of the Department of Sociology at Minot State University in North Dakota also showed that stressed pregnancies equal gay babies. If the foetus is a girl, a baby daughter may become super-feminine and will probably have poor spatial ability. In other words, she's very mothering and nurturing but can't reverse park or find North. Brian Gladue of North Dakota State University has shown that heterosexual men have better spatial skills than homosexual men, and lesbians have better spatial skills than heterosexual women. Why? More male hormone was involved in the wiring of their brains. So what suppresses testosterone? The main factors are stress, sickness and some medications.

We have known for some time about the dangerous effects of alcohol and nicotine on the unborn baby and of the positive effects of the right diet and stress-free living. New research by experts such as Dr Vivette Glover at London's Chelsea Hospital shows that pregnant women who suffer stress give birth to babies who are also unable to deal with stressful situations. Dr Glenn Wilson of the Institute of Psychiatry in London has also studied this area extensively. He concluded, 'Certain chemical drugs can interfere with testosterone function and the result can be the birth of a gay baby.'

If the foetus is a genetic girl (XX) and the brain is dosed in male hormone, the result is a female body with male brain circuitry. As children, these girls are usually called 'tomboys' and they play rougher and harder than their female peers. They are likely to grow more body and facial hair than other girls at puberty, they are better at hand-eye and ball skills and as adults are sometimes described as 'butch'. A high percentage become lesbians. Accidental dosing of male hormones can occur if the pregnant mother is taking certain medications that contain high levels of male hormones, like some contraceptive pills, diabetic drugs and other medications.

One study of diabetic women who were pregnant during the 1950s and '60s shows a high ratio of baby girls who became lesbians after adolescence because their brains received too much male hormone from the diabetic drug at the critical period of brain development of the foetus.

Similarly, another study showed that women of the same era who received female hormones such as oestrogen in the belief that it would help pregnancy had a five to ten times greater chance of giving birth to a gay baby boy. It's not until adolescence that the brain circuitry is switched on by the massive surge of hormones that race through a teenager's body and the real sexuality of the teenager becomes apparent.

Echoing these findings, researchers at the Kinsey Institute in America found that mothers who had taken male hormones during pregnancy had daughters who were described as having high levels of self-reliance, self-assertiveness and were likely to be involved in aggressive sports such as kickboxing or football. As children, many were described as 'tomboys'. Mothers who had taken female hormones had more daughters who were described as more 'feminine' and sons who were softer and gentler than their peers, were more dependent on others and were not physically active.

The Transsexual Brain

Transsexuals feel from early childhood that they were born in the wrong-sex body. The area in the brain essential for sexual behaviour is called the hypothalamus and this area is markedly smaller in women than in men. Researcher Dick Swaab and his team from the Netherlands Institute for Brain Research were the first in 1995 to show that the hypothalamus in male transsexuals was female-sized or smaller. This further confirms research showing that gender identity stems from an interaction between the developing brain and sex hormones. This theory was first proposed by German scientist Dr Gunther Dörner who found that the hypothalamus of homosexual men responded in the exact same way as a female hypothalamus when injected with female hormone. Swaab reported, 'Our study is the first to show a female brain structure in genetically male transsexuals.' In other words, it's a woman's brain trapped in a man's body.

The psychiatric label for a transgender person is that they are suffering Gender Identity Disorder and around 20% of these people undergo the sex-change operation. This involves removing the testicles and cutting the penis in half lengthways and removing the inside tissue. The penis skin remains attached, the urethral tube is realigned and the skin from the penis is then folded inside a surgically made cavity to line an artificial vagina. In some cases, the head of the penis becomes the clitoris and is capable of orgasm. Tragically, the suicide rate for transsexuals is five times that of the general population. One in five attempt suicide.

Are We Slaves to Our Biology?

Scientists know how to change the sexuality of rats and monkeys in the womb. Some groups claim that we can control our likes and dislikes by will or choice and they insist that we can all reverse park or read street directories with the same ease. But scientists know this is unrealistic. You don't need to be a scientist to see that rabbits can't fly, ducks are lousy runners, most women have difficulty reading maps and men reading newspapers are temporarily deaf. Understanding brain structure differences makes us more tolerant of each other and allows us to have greater control over our destiny and to feel positive about our inclinations and choices.

Human intelligence has evolved to a point where we are more in control of our emotions than other animals and can think through our choices. Other animals don't think: they react to circumstances and this makes them slaves to their biology. Our biology is the motivation behind many of the choices we make that sometimes don't seem to make sense to us. So while we are more in control of ourselves than most other animals, we still can't completely buck the system. The biggest obstacle facing most people is their rejection of the idea that we are just another animal with a smart brain. This refusal makes these people victims of their biology.

Why Gay Men Aren't All Alike

In simple terms, there are two main centres associated with homosexual behaviour, the 'mating centre' and the 'behaviour centre'.

The 'mating centre' is located in the hypothalamus and decides which sex we will be attracted to. In males, it needs to be dosed in male hormones to convert it to male operational function, so that a man will be attracted to a woman. If it receives insufficient male hormones it will remain, to a greater or lesser extent, female in operation and so the man will be attracted to other men.

The 'behaviour centre' in the brain may not, however, receive enough male hormones to give a man masculine behaviour, speech and body language. If it doesn't receive enough for male reconfiguration, the man's behaviour will be significantly feminine.

How the mating and behaviour centres can receive different amounts of male hormone is still a mystery, but it certainly demonstrates why not all effeminate males are gay, and not all macho men are heterosexual.

Lesbian Differences

If the brain of a female foetus inadvertently receives additional male hormones, it can masculinise the mating centre.

This means that as a woman she will be attracted to other women. If her behaviour centre is also masculinised, she will take on masculine behaviour, speech and body language, and may be described as 'butch'.

If her behaviour centre is not converted by male hormones, on the other hand, she will remain feminine in behaviour, but will still be attracted to other females. These results have also been shown in experiments on female rats and monkeys.

While 'butch' lesbians can be plainly seen to be the result of their biology, many people today still resist the idea that feminine lesbians are also prisoners of their make-up. They suggest these women must have actually *chosen* to be gay, because they most definitely do not look gay. Just witness the number of men who say, when they see a very feminine, or 'lipstick', lesbian, 'I bet I could get her to change her mind'.

These women, however, really are attracted to other women.

CHAPTER 9
MEN, WOMEN AND SEX

Stella and Jeremy met at the party of a mutual friend. The attraction was instant and spilled over immediately into a fast and furious relationship. They were both smitten and physically couldn't get enough of each other. Their speciality was House Sex – sex in the living-room, the bedroom, kitchen, bathroom, on the staircase and in the garage. For Jeremy, the sex was great, so he decided that Stella was the one for him. It was wonderful for Stella too, so she decided she must be in love. They were going to live together, forever.

Two years later, their sex life was still fast and furious – he was fast and she was furious. Stella was happy with sex twice a week, but Jeremy wanted it every day. After all, he'd given up single life for this relationship so he felt it was a fair trade-off. The more he insisted on sex, the less she wanted it, and soon they were having only Bedroom Sex. They started to fight over little things, the kisses and cuddles slowly disappeared from their everyday life and they were soon seeing only negatives in each other. They even began going to bed at different times and avoided each other. Now, all they had was Hallway Sex – they'd pass in the hallway and shout, 'Screw You!' One lonely night, one of them went to a mutual friend's party and met someone. The attraction was instant and spilled over immediately into a fast and furious relationship. They were both smitten and physically couldn't get enough ...

How Sex Began

Life began with a single-cell creature about 3.5 billion years ago. To survive, it divided itself to make exact copies. It thus remained the same for millions of years and only changed its appearance if, by accident, a mutation in its structure occurred or it learned something new by experience. Life was slow.

Then, about 800 million years ago, the cell learned an amazing trick, again probably by accident. It somehow figured out how to trade genes with other cells. This meant that any survival advantages the other cell had acquired could be passed immediately to a new baby cell, making it stronger and more resilient than its parents. It was now no longer necessary to wait millions of years for an accident to mutate the cell towards better survival.

This was an enormously successful development that accelerated the growth of new cells towards bigger and better things at a staggering rate of speed, beginning with the soft-bodied creatures like worms and jellyfish. Six hundred million years ago came animals with bones and shells, and 300 million years later, the first fish learned to breathe and dragged themselves on to the land. And all as a result of gene trading.

Sex was now in full flight. Once the new cell was created with its stronger genes it was necessary that the parents died. This was for two reasons. Firstly, the new cell was better than the parent cells so the parents were unnecessary. Secondly, the parents needed to be removed so that they did not breed with the new cell and thus, weaken it. Death meant that the new, stronger gene could survive and share its genes with other new survivors. So the original purpose of sex was to trade genes with someone else to create stronger genes in the next generation of babies. For most of our history, however, no connection was ever made between sex and babies, and there are still several primitive tribes who have not yet made this connection.

Where is Sex in the Brain?

Your sex centre is located in the hypothalamus which is the part of the brain that also controls the emotions, heart rate and blood pressure. It's about the size of a cherry and weighs around 4.5 grams and is larger in men than in women, homosexuals and transsexuals.

This is the area in which hormones, particularly testosterone, stimulate the desire for sex. Considering that men have 10 to 20 times more testosterone than women and a larger hypothalamus, it's obvious why the male sex drive is so powerful. This is the reason men can have sex virtually any time and in almost any place. Add to this the social encouragement that men have received for generations to 'sow their oats' and society's disapproval of sexually active women, and it's little wonder the differences in attitude to sex have always been a bone of contention between men and women (no pun intended).

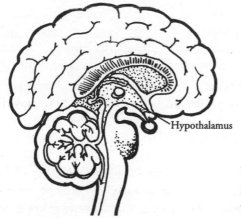

Hypothalamus

The brain's
sex centre –
the hypothalamus

Why Men Can't Help Themselves

Men's enthusiastic and impulsive sex drive has a clear purpose – to ensure that the human species continues. Like most male mammals, he had to evolve with several elements for its success. Firstly, his sex drive had to be intensely focused and not easily distracted. This would allow him to have sex under almost any conditions, such as in the presence of potential threatening enemies, or in any place where a sexual opportunity presented itself.

A man needed to be able to ejaculate as often as possible in the shortest space of time to avoid being caught by predators or enemies.

He also needed to spread his seed as far afield and as often as possible. The Kinsey Institute in the US, world leaders in human sex research, reported that, without society's social rules, they believe nearly all men would be promiscuous, as 80% of all human societies have been for most of human existence. Since the arrival of the age of monogamy, however, men's biological urge has caused constant mayhem for couples trying to build a relationship and is the number one cause of modern relationship problems.

Why Women Are Faithful

A woman's hypothalamus is much smaller than a man's and she only has small amounts of testosterone to activate it. This is why women, overall, have significantly lower sex drives than men and are less aggressive. So why didn't nature create woman as a raving nymphomaniac to ensure continuation of the species? The answer is in the long period of time it takes to conceive and to raise a child to self-sufficiency.

In species such as rabbits, for example, the gestation period is only six weeks and the newborn bunnies are capable of feeding themselves, running and hiding within two weeks. There is no need for father rabbit to be there to defend or feed them. A newborn elephant or fallow deer is able to run with the herd shortly after they are born. Even our closest cousin, the chimpanzee, will survive if orphaned after six months. For a significant part of the nine-month human pregnancy period, most women are physically restricted and it takes at least five years before a human child can feed and defend itself. For this reason, women closely analyse a potential father's traits such as his ability to provide food and shelter and fight off enemies.

Some men think that parenting

ends with conception.

A woman's brain is programmed to find a man who will make a commitment to being around long enough to rear her children. This is reflected in what women look for in a long-term partner.

Men Are Microwaves, Women Are Electric Ovens

Male sex drive is like a microwave – it ignites instantly and operates at full capacity within seconds, and can be turned off just as quickly when the meal is cooked. Women's sex drive is like an electric oven – it heats slowly to its top temperature and takes a lot longer to cool down.

The following graph shows the sex drives of average men and women throughout their lifetimes. It has not been adjusted to reflect the various periods in life where drives may be higher or lower based on environmental factors such as births, deaths, courtship, retirement, and so on. To demonstrate sex drive differences we've simplified this graph to illustrate the differences.

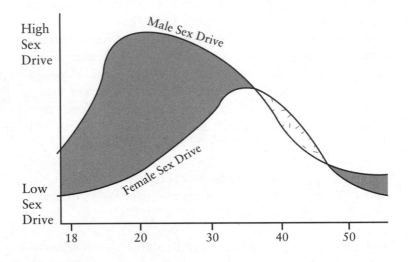

Male and female sex drive

A man's testosterone level slowly decreases as he gets older and his sex drive decreases accordingly. The average woman's sex drive gradually increases so that her sexual peak is between the ages of 36–38, which explains the 'toy boy' syndrome of the older woman/younger man. Younger men have the physical performance level an older woman craves. A man's sexual performance level at age 19 is more compatible with a woman in her late 30s to early 40s. You will also notice on the chart that the sex drive of a man in his 40s is compatible with a woman in her early 20s which partly explains the older man/younger woman combination. There is usually a 10 to 20–year age difference between these older/younger combinations.

When we say a man's sex drive peaks at age 19 and falls in later life, we are talking about his physical performance level. His interest in sex is usually high for most of his life, meaning that he can be just as interested at 70 as he was at 30 but his performance level is not as high. A woman can be very interested in sex in her late teens (because of its relationship to love) but feel limited desire for sex. She can have the same interest in her 30s but at that time she also has a greater desire for it.

Why We Argue About Sex

Bear in mind that we are talking here about the overall sex drive of all men as one group and all women as another. Individual sex drives vary from person to person, but in this chapter we are discussing the typical drives of most people.

An individual woman may have a high sex drive and a man may have a low drive, but these are minority cases and do not reflect the vast majority. Overall, most men have a higher sex drive than most women. A study at the Kinsey Institute showed that 37% of men think about sex every 30 minutes. Only 11% of women think of it as often. For a man, a continual high dose of testosterone keeps his drive high and this is why, when it comes to sex, he's ever ready.

When it comes to sex, women

need a reason; men need a place.

The shaded areas on the graph are where most men and women argue about sex. Until her late 30s, a woman will complain that a man constantly puts pressure on her for sex, causing resentment on both sides. She will often accuse him of 'using' her. It's not until her late 30s that a woman's sex drive matches a man's, and often surpasses it. Her drive is nature's way of pushing her into last minute childbearing urges before the onset of menopause. A man in his early 40s can often be caught by surprise by this role reversal. His sex drive may be lower than a woman's of the same age while her level of assertiveness may be higher. Many men complain about having to 'perform on demand'. The boot is now on the other foot, so to speak. We recommend you read *Good Loving, Great Sex* by Dr Rosie King and *Mars And Venus In The Bedroom* by Dr John Gray. Both books offer excellent techniques and strategies for handling sex drive differences. Most couples don't address these differences and each expects the other to understand their needs, but that's not how nature planned it.

Men and women have different sex drives, and most couples experience different levels of sex drive at different times in their week, month and year. It may be fashionable to suggest that modern men and women are equally interested in sex, or that normal couples are perfectly matched sexually, but that's not the way it is in real life.

Despite what the poets write and the romantics might think, sex drive results from the cocktail of hormones released by the brain. Testosterone is the main hormone that creates the feeling we call sex drive and, as discussed in Chapter 7, love is a combination of chemical and electrical reactions. Those who think that love is all in the mind are partially correct. For women, the psychological factors such as trust, closeness and overall well-being all combine to create the conditions under which the hormone cocktail is released by the brain. Men can release this cocktail any time, any place.

Studies carried out on American University campuses showed that when an attractive woman approaches a man and asks him to go to bed with her, 75% say yes, whereas no women said yes when approached by an attractive man.

Sex Drive and Stress

A woman's sex drive is significantly affected by events in her life. If she hates her job, she has a really demanding project at work, the mortgage repayments have just doubled, the kids are sick, she was drenched in the rain or the dog ran away, sex will not even be a consideration. All she can think about is going to bed and sleeping.

When the same events happen to a man, he sees sex as a sleeping pill – a way of releasing the built-up tensions of the day. So, at the end of the day, he puts the hard word on the woman, she calls him an insensitive moron, he calls her frigid and he gets to sleep on the couch. Sound familiar? Interestingly, when men are asked about the state of their relationship they usually discuss it in terms of their partner's personal services on the day they were asked, for example, whether she cooked him breakfast, ironed his shirt or massaged his head. Women describe the condition of the relationship based on recent events, for example, how attentive he's been over the last few months, his helpfulness around the house and how much he has communicated with her. Most men don't understand this difference. He may have been a perfect gentleman all day but she refuses sex because she's still unhappy that he insulted her mother two weeks ago.

One remarkable study found that the level of criticism and contempt displayed by a couple towards each other bears a direct relation to the number of infectious diseases from which they would suffer over the next five years, especially in the women. The higher the level of criticism, the more prevalent and virulent the infections. The reason for this is that heightened stress levels resulting from arguments weakens the immune system, making the body more susceptible to disease and less able to cope.

How Much Sex Are We Having?

A survey of couples conducted in Australia in 2000 showed the average frequency of sex for couples. Those who participated in the survey were chosen at random and it was conducted anonymously so it is likely respondents were telling the truth.

Age	Frequency of Sex
20s	148 times a year
30s	110 times a year
40s	78 times a year
50s	61 times a year
60s	61 times a year

Keep in mind that these are averages. Some 65–year–olds go at it six times a week and some 20–year–olds have never had sex, but these are exceptions rather than the rule. Interestingly, 81% of couples claimed to be happy with their sex life which, assuming they were telling the truth, means that plenty of negotiation must have been taking place to make up for the excess of men's sex drive. The percentage of couples who say they have a satisfactory sex life in Western countries usually runs at around 60%.

One American study found that all white men have roughly the same amount of sex, Latin women have sex more often than black or white women (who have about the same amount), and black women are 50% more likely than white women to reach orgasm every time they have sex. Asian men were found to be having the least amount of sex which is consistent with their lower testoterone levels.

Sex on the Brain

American Demographics magazine reported the findings of a group of researchers who surveyed over 10,000 adults in 1997 and discovered a link between sex drive and intelligence. They found that the cleverer you are, the less sex you have, or want to have. Intellectuals with postgraduate qualifications had sex 52 times a year compared to an average of 61 times for ordinary graduates, while school leavers averaged 59 times. Men with nine-to-five jobs had sex 48 times a year, compared to 82 times for men working more than 60 hours a week – increased testosterone probably made the difference to both their work drive and sex drive. Jazz enthusiasts have sex 34% more than those who like pop, and classical enthusiasts have the least sex.

A woman is most safe with a Chinese man who loves classical music and works part-time, but she should beware of hardworking jazz pianists.

For men, testosterone comes in five to seven waves a day, and is highest at sunrise – up to twice as high as at any other time in the day – just before he sets out for the day's hunting. On average, a man's testosterone is 30% lower in the evening when he's fire-gazing.

'I woke up at 6 o'clock one morning and my wife was

poking me in the back with a broom handle!', one man told us after a lecture we had given. 'When I asked her what she was doing, she said, "You try it for a change!"'

How Sex Improves Your Health

There is an overwhelming amount of evidence that sex is great for your health. Having an amorous interlude an average of three times a week burns up 35,000 kilojoules, which is equal to running 130 kilometres in a year. Sex increases your testosterone levels which fortify your bones and muscles and supply you with good cholesterol. Sex researcher Dr Beverley Whipple says, 'Endorphins, which are the body's natural pain killers, are released during sex and are good for relieving headache, whiplash and arthritis.'

The hormone DHEA (dehydroepiandrosterone) is also released just prior to orgasm, and improves cognition, builds the immune system, inhibits tumour growth and builds bones. In a woman, oxytocin, the hormone that arouses the desire to be touched, is released in large doses during sex and her oestrogen levels also increase. Dr Harold Bloomfield, in his book *The Power of Five*, showed how oestrogen is associated with better bones and a better cardiovascular system in women. The effect of all these hormones is to protect the heart and extend life, so more sex equals longer life and less stress. The list of benefits for having a vibrant sex life is getting longer and longer!

Monogamy and Polygamy

Polygamy is where a man or woman has more than one partner at one time. By now you may have reached the conclusion that the human species is not monogamous by nature. Certainly, during most of our evolution, more than 80% of all human societies were polygamous societies, mainly for survival reasons.

Some men think monogamy is

what furniture is made out of.

Monogamy means that one male is permanently paired with one female, which is the natural state for a number of animal species, such as foxes, geese and eagles. Monogamous male and female animals are generally the same physical size and parenting responsibilities are divided 50/50. In polygamous species, the males are usually bigger, more colourful, more aggressive and have minimal involvement in parenting. The males of polygamous animals mature sexually much later than the females so that competitive conflicts are avoided between the older males and younger, inexperienced males who are less likely to survive a fight. Human males fit the physical specifications of polygamous species; it's no wonder men have a constant battle to stay monogamous.

Why Men Are Promiscuous

Where does marriage fit into the lifestyle of an animal species that has a biologically promiscuous male?

Promiscuity is wired into a man's brain and is a legacy of his evolutionary past. Throughout human history, wars greatly diminished the numbers of men so it made sense to add to the size of the tribe as often as possible. The number of men returning from battle was usually lower than at the start. This meant that there was always a large number of widows, so creating a harem for the returning males was an effective survival strategy for the tribe.

Giving birth to boys was seen as a wonderful event because additional males were always needed to defend the community. Girls were a disappointment because the tribe invariably had an excess of females. This is the way it was for hundreds of thousands of years. In addition, modern man is still equipped with a large hypothalamus and enormous amounts of testosterone to fulfil his ancient urge to procreate. The reality is that men, like most primates and other mammals, are not biologically inclined to complete monogamy.

The huge male-oriented sex industry offers pertinent proof. Practically all pornography, erotic videos, prostitution and X-rated Internet images are directed at men, showing that while most men can live in a monogamous relationship, their brain-wiring demands polygamous mental stimulation. It has to be understood, however, that in discussing men's urge to be promiscuous, we are talking about biological *inclinations*. We are not promoting promiscuous behaviour or providing men with an excuse for infidelity. We live today in a world that is completely different to that of our past, and our own biology is often completely at odds with our expectations and demands.

Human biology is
dangerously out of date.

The fact that something may be instinctive or natural doesn't mean that it's good for us. The brain circuitry of a moth gives it an instinctive attraction towards bright lights and this allows the moth to navigate at night using the stars and the moon. Unfortunately, the modern moth is also living in a world that is dramatically different to the one in which it evolved. We now have moth and mosquito zappers. By doing what is natural and instinctive, the modern moth flies into the zapper and is incinerated instantly. In understanding their biological urges, modern men have a choice of avoiding self-incineration as a result of doing what comes naturally.

There's a small percentage of women who are as promiscuous as men, but their motivation is usually different to that of men. To be turned on sexually, the brain circuitry of the nest-defending human female responds to a range of criteria other than just the promise of sex. Most women want a relationship or at least the possibility of some emotional connection before they feel the desire for sex. Most men don't realise that once a woman feels an emotional bond has been created, she will happily bonk his brains out for the next three to six months. With the exception of the rare percentage of nymphomaniacs, most women feel the strongest urge for physical sex during ovulation which can last several days or several hours.

If unrestrained, most men would fall into a bottomless pit of mindless fornication to guarantee survival of the tribe. A survey conducted by the American Health Institute showed that 82% of boys aged 16–19 said they liked the idea of participating in an orgy with strangers, while only two percent of girls felt the same. The rest found the idea appalling.

A woman wants lots of sex with the man she loves. A man wants lots of sex.

The Rooster Effect

A rooster is a very randy male bird which can copulate with hens almost incessantly, more than 60 times in a given mating. He cannot, however, mate with the same hen more than five times in one day. By the sixth time, he completely loses interest and can't 'get it up' but, if he is presented with a new hen, he can mount her with the same enthusiasm he did with the first. This is known as the 'Rooster Effect'.

A bull will lose interest after copulating seven times with the same cow but can be fired up again by the introduction of a new one. By the time he reaches the tenth new cow, he is still giving an impressive performance.

A ram will not mount the same ewe more than five times, but can continue to mount new ewes with tremendous zeal. Even when the ram's former sexual partners are disguised with perfume or bags over their heads, the ram still cannot perform. You just can't fool them. This is nature's way of ensuring that the male's seed is spread as widely as possible in order to achieve the highest number of conceptions and ensure the survival of that species.

Men give their penis a name because

they don't want a stranger making

99% of their decisions for them.

For healthy young men, that number is also around five. On a good day, he can have sex with the same woman five times but will usually fail to give a sixth encore. Introduce a new female however, and, like roosters and bulls, his interest (along with parts of his anatomy) can rapidly rise.

Male sex urge is so strong that Dr Patrick Carnes of the Sexual Recovery Institute in Los Angeles estimates that up to eight percent of men are addicted to sex, compared to less than three percent of women.

Why Men Want Women to Dress Like Tarts (But Never in Public)

A man's brain needs variety. Like most male mammals, a man is pre-wired to seek out and mate with as many healthy females as possible. This is why men love novelty factors like sexy lingerie in a monogamous relationship. Unlike other mammals, men can fool themselves into believing they have a harem of different women by dressing their partners in a range of sexy clothing and lingerie. It is, in effect, his version of putting a bag over her head to provide a variety of different appearances. Most women know the effect lingerie has on men although few understand why it is so powerful.

Every Christmas the lingerie sections of department stores are full of men sheepishly skulking around trying to find a sexy gift for their partners. In January, those women are standing in line at the refunds counter in the same store. 'This is just not me,' they say, 'he wants me to dress up like a hooker!' The hooker is, however, a professional sex seller who has researched market demands and is packaged to make a sale. One American study has shown that women who wear a variety of erotic lingerie have generally much more faithful men than women who prefer white cotton underwear. This is just one way that a man's urge for variety is sometimes addressed in a monogamous relationship.

Why Men Are Three-Minute Wonders

From a cold start to orgasm, a healthy man's average time is around two-and-a-half minutes. For a healthy woman, the same average is 13 minutes. For most mammals, copulation is a fast affair because when they are preoccupied with being joined together, they are vulnerable to attack from predators. The quickie was Nature's way of preserving the species.

'You're a lousy lover!' she said. 'How can

you tell that in two minutes?' he asked.

Depending on age, health and mood, many men can have sex several times a day, sustaining an erection for varying lengths of time. This is much more impressive than the male African baboon which mates for between merely ten and 20 seconds, and gives just four to eight pelvic thrusts per mating, but pales into insignificance against the wild rat, which has been recorded mating up to 400 times in a ten-hour period. But first place in the animal kingdom goes to the Shaw's mouse, which holds the current sexual record of more than 100 matings per hour.

The Ball Game

'It takes a lot of balls to do that!' This is a common expression that highlights how we unconsciously recognise the relationship between testicle size and assertiveness. Right across the animal world, testes size – relative to the owner's overall body mass – is the main factor in determining testosterone levels. Testes size is not necessarily related to body size, however. A gorilla, for example, weighs four times more than a chimpanzee but a chimp's testicles are four times heavier than a gorilla's. A sparrow's testicles are eight times larger, relative to its body mass, than an eagle's testicles, making the sparrow one of the randiest little guys around. Now here's the point: testicle size determines the male's level of faithfulness or monogamy. The African

Bonobo chimpanzee has the largest testicles of all primates and has sex incessantly with every female in sight, but the mighty gorilla, with his relatively small balls, would be lucky to have sex once a year, even though he has his own harem. On the testicle/body mass ratio, human males have balls that are an average size for primates. This means that men produce enough testosterone to encourage them to be promiscuous, but little enough to be kept monogamous with strict rules enforced by women, religion or the society in which they live.

In light of all this, it would make sense if political leaders like Bill Clinton, John F. Kennedy, Winston Churchill and Saddam Hussein had larger than average balls, although we haven't actually got close enough to check. It also follows that their sex drive would then be correspondingly much higher than the average man's and would need an outlet. The public puts big-balled, high-testosterone individuals into positions of power and then expects them to behave with as much sexual restraint as a neutered cat. The reality is that high sex drives get them into positions of power and can then, ironically, see them turfed them out again.

Ray plays his wedding video backward.

He says it's so he can see himself

walk out of church, a free man.

There may soon be a solution to the philandering urges of males. In 1999, Drs Larry Young and Thomas Insel of Emory University in Atlanta, carried out studies on two groups of rodents known as voles. They used two types of vole: monogamous prairie voles and their polygamous cousins, the montane vole, which share 99% of the same genes. In *Nature* Magazine, Young and Insel described how they took the gene (called the vasopressin receptor gene) that plays a role in male behaviours, including aggression, communication, sexual activity, and social memory, from a monogamous vole and inserted it into the polygamous vole. They discovered that the resulting 'new mice' formed close relationships with females and behaved in many other monogamous ways.

There is only one guaranteed solution to the problem of male infidelity – castration. Not only would a man be monogamous, he wouldn't have to shave much, he wouldn't go bald and he'd live longer. Studies of men in mental institutions show that castrated men live to an average age of 69, while men left intact with testosterone coursing through their bodies only live to 56. The same principle applies to your cat.

We can also expect future generations of men to be much less potent than modern men. Testicle size and sperm production have been steadily decreasing for generations. Evidence shows that our male ancestors had much larger balls than modern men and, compared to other primates, men produce significantly smaller amounts of sperm per gram of tissue than their gorilla or chimp cousins. The average sperm count of men is now approximately half that of men in the 1940s so we are now producing males who are less masculine than their grandfathers.

Balls Have Brains Too

Dr Robin Baker from the School of Biological Sciences at the University of Manchester conducted some remarkable research that showed a man's brain can unconsciously sense from a woman's behaviour when her ovulation stage has arrived. His body then calculates and releases the exact amount of sperm required at any given moment to create the greatest chance of conception. For example, if a couple is having sex every day, around the woman's ovulation time his body may release 100 million sperm per session. If he hasn't seen her for three days, his body will release 300 million sperm in a session, and 500 million if he has not seen her for five days – even if he has been having sex every day with other women. Based on biological calculations by his brain, his body releases just enough to do the job of conception and fight off any other competitive sperm that may be present.

Men and Ogling

Men are stimulated through their eyes, women through their ears. Men's brains are wired to look at female shapes and this is why erotic images have so much impact on them. Women, with their greater range of sensory information receptors, want to hear sweet words. A woman's sensitivity to hearing wonderful compliments is so strong, many women even close their eyes when their lover whispers sweet nothings.

Miss Universe contests command large audiences of both men and women but television polls show there are more male viewers than female. This is because men are attracted to the female form and these contests are an acceptable form of male ogling. By contrast, Mr Universe contests appeal to almost no-one and are rarely televised. This is because neither men or women are interested in the passive male form because the attractiveness of a man usually depends on his skills and physical prowess.

Miss Universe competitions are watched

mainly by men, but Mr Universe

contests turn nobody on.

When a woman with a nice body walks by, a man, lacking as he does good peripheral vision, turns his head to look and goes into a trance-like state. His blinking ceases and saliva fills his mouth, a reaction described by women as 'drooling'. If a couple are walking down the street and Miss Mini Skirt comes swaying towards them on the other side of the street, the woman's short-range peripheral vision allows her to spot the woman before the man does. She'll make quick comparisons between herself and the potential competitor, usually negative ones against herself. When the man eventually spots her he receives a negative reaction from his woman for ogling. A woman will usually have two negative thoughts in this situation: firstly, she mistakenly thinks that the man may prefer to be with the other woman than with her and, secondly, that she is not as physically attractive as the other woman. Men are attracted visually to curves, leg lengths, and shapes. *Any* woman with the right shape and proportions will catch his attention.

Men prefer looks to brains because most men can see better than they can think.

It doesn't mean that the man immediately wants to race the other woman off to bed, but it is a reminder to him that he is masculine and his evolutionary role is to look for opportunities to increase the size of the tribe. After all, he doesn't even know the other woman and could not realistically be thinking about a long-term relationship with her. This same principle applies to a man looking at the centrefold in a men's magazine. When he looks at the naked woman, he doesn't wonder if she has a nice personality, can cook or play the piano. He looks at the shapes, curves and her physical equipment – that's all. For him it's not much different to admiring a leg of ham hanging in a shop window. We are not making excuses for the rude, blatant ogling that some men do; we're simply explaining that if a man gets caught ogling, it doesn't mean he doesn't love his partner – it's his biology at work. It's also interesting to note that in a public place like the beach or swimming pool, studies show that women ogle more than men. Being equipped with better peripheral vision, women rarely get caught.

What Men Need to Do

One of the best compliments a man can pay a woman is not to 'ogle' inappropriately at another female, particularly in public, but to give his partner a simultaneous compliment. For example, 'Sure, she's got great legs, but I'll bet she doesn't have a great sense of humour ... she's not in the same league as you, darling.' When this type of complimentary approach is used in the presence of other people, especially her friends, it pays big dividends to the man with the courage to try it. Women need to understand that a man is biologically compelled to look at certain female shapes and curves, and that they shouldn't feel threatened by it. An easy way for a woman to take the pressure off a man is for her to notice the other woman first and make the first comment. A man also needs to understand that no woman appreciates inappropriate ogling.

What We Really Want, Long-Term

This chart is of a survey of more than 15,000 men and women aged 17–60 which shows, in order of importance, what women are looking for in a long-term sexual partner and what men *think* women want.

A
What Women Look For
1. Personality
2. Humour
3. Sensitivity
4. Brains
5. Good body

B
What Men Think Women Look For
1. Personality
2. Good body
3. Humour
4. Sensitivity
5. Good looks

This study shows that men have a reasonable understanding of what a woman wants in a man. Men placed 'Good body' high on list B but this was not high on a woman's criteria list. And 15% of men believed that having a large penis was important to a woman but only two percent of women said that it mattered. Some men are so convinced that penis size is critical that penis extension equipment is now sold in sex shops and magazines everywhere.

Now let's look at what men want in a long-term sexual partner and what women *think* they want.

C
What Men Look For
1. Personality
2. Good looks
3. Brains
4. Humour
5. Good body

D
What Women Think Men Look For
1. Good looks
2. Good body
3. Breasts
4. Bum
5. Personality

As you can see, women are considerably less aware of men's criteria for a long-term partner. This is because women base their assumptions on the behavioural traits they see or hear in men – men gaping at women's bodies. List A is both a short-term and long-term criteria list for what a women wants in a man but for a man, things are different. List D is what a man looks for when he first meets a woman, but List C is what he really looks for in the long-term.

Why Men Want 'Just One Thing'

Men want sex; women want love. This has been known for thousands of years but why it is so, and what to do about it, is rarely a topic of conversation. It is a major source of complaint and argument between men and women. Ask most women what they want in a man and they will normally say they like a man with broad shoulders, a small waist, and good arms and legs – all the equipment needed to catch or wrestle large animals – plus he must be caring, gentle and sensitive to her needs, and a good conversationalist, which are all female attributes. Unfortunately for most women, the combination of manly body and female values is usually found only in gay or effeminate men.

A man needs to be trained in the art of pleasuring a woman as it does not come naturally to him. He's a hunter – he's wired to solve problems, chase lunch and fight enemies. At the end of the day, he just wants to fire-gaze and give a few pelvic thrusts to keep his tribe populated. For a woman to feel the desire for sex she needs to feel loved, adored and significant. Now here's the twist that most people never realise: A man needs to have sex before he can get in tune with his feelings. Unfortunately, a woman needs him to do that first before she's turned on to sex. A man is wired to hunt. His body is conditioned to do this regardless of freezing, icy, hot or sweltering conditions. His skin is desensitised so that he is not handicapped by injuries, burns or chills. Historically, a man's world was full of fighting and death – there was no place for sensitivity to others' needs, communications or feelings. To spend time communicating or expressing compassion meant a man would lose concentration and leave the tribe open to attack. A woman needs to understand that this is the biology with which modern males are saddled, and devise appropriate strategies to deal with it.

Women are taught by their mothers that men want 'just one thing' – sex – but this is not completely accurate. Men want love, but they can only get it *through* sex.

The sexual priorities of men and women are so opposite that it makes no sense for either to chastise the other. Neither one can help it; it's just the way they were made. Besides, being opposites is one of the things that attract. It's only in two gay male or female partners that sexual desires are usually the same, which is why homosexual men and women don't have the love/sex argument as often as heterosexuals.

Why Sex Suddenly Stops

The person who first said that the way to a man's heart is through his stomach was aiming too high. After a man has had great sex, his softer, feminine side emerges. He can hear birds singing, is struck by the colours of the trees, can smell the flowers and is touched by the words of a song. Before sex, he probably only noticed the birds because of the mess they made on his car. But a man needs to understand this after-sex side is the one that a woman loves to see and finds wonderfully seductive. If he can practise feeling this way, he'll be able to turn the woman on before having sex. At the same time, a woman needs to understand the importance of giving great sex to a man so she can glimpse this softer side and explain how alluring she finds it.

At the beginning of a new relationship, sex is always great and there is plenty of love. She gives him plenty of sex and he gives her plenty of love, and one thing feeds the other. After a few years, however, the man becomes preoccupied with lunch-chasing and the woman with nest-defending, which is why sex and love seem to stop simultaneously. Men and women are equally responsible for whether they have a good or bad sex life, but each often blames the other when things don't go well. Men need to understand that a woman needs attention, praise, pampering and lots of time before she heats her electric oven. Women have to remember that these are the feelings men are more likely to express *after* a session of great sex. A man should remember how he felt after sex, and relive these feelings with a woman when he wants sex next time. A woman should be prepared to help him.

The key here is sex. For when sex is great, the whole relationship dramatically improves.

How To Satisfy A Woman Every Time:

Caress, praise, pamper, relish, savour, massage, fix things, empathise, serenade, compliment, support, feed, soothe, tantalise, humour, placate, stimulate, stroke, console, hug, ignore fat bits, cuddle, excite, pacify, protect, phone, anticipate, smooch, nuzzle, forgive, accessorise, entertain, charm, carry for, oblige, fascinate, attend to, trust, defend, clothe, brag about, sanctify, acknowledge, spoil, embrace, die for, dream of, tease, gratify, squeeze, indulge, idolise, worship.

How To Satisfy A Man Every Time:

Arrive naked.

What Men Want From Sex

For men this is simple: the release of built-up tension by orgasm. After sex a man weighs less (some say it's because his brain is empty) because he has lost a part of his body and he needs rest to recover. This is why men often fall asleep after sex. A woman may become angry about this and feel that he is selfish or doesn't care about her needs.

Men also use sex to express physically what they can't

express emotionally. If a man has a problem such as how he'll find a new job, pay the overdraft or resolve a dispute, he's likely to use sex to relieve the intensity of his emotions. Women usually don't understand this and become resentful at being 'used', missing the point that the man had a problem he couldn't deal with.

Men fantasise about having sex with two women. Women fantasise about it too – so that they'll have someone to talk to when he falls asleep.

There are few problems a man can have that great sex won't fix. Tests show that a man who has a pent-up need for sex has difficulty hearing, thinking, driving or operating heavy machinery. He also suffers a form of time-distortion where 3 minutes feels like 15. If a woman wants an intelligent decision from a man she's better off discussing it after sex, when his brain is clear.

What Women Want From Sex

For a man to feel fulfilled through sex, he needs the release of tension. A woman has the opposite need: she needs to feel the build-up of tension over a longer period of time with her prerequisite of lots of attention and talk. He wants to empty; she wants to fill up. Understanding this difference makes men more caring lovers. Most women need at least 30 minutes of foreplay before they are ready for sex. Men need at least 30 seconds, and most consider driving back to her place as foreplay.

Adam came first – but men usually do.

After sex, a woman is high on hormones and is ready to take on the world. She wants to touch, cuddle and talk. A man, however, if he hasn't already fallen asleep, sometimes withdraws by getting up and 'doing something' such as changing a lightbulb or making coffee. This is because a man needs to feel in control of himself at all times and, during orgasm, he temporarily loses control. Getting up and doing something allows him to regain that command.

Why Men Don't Talk During Sex

Most men can only do one thing at a time. When a man has an erection he finds it difficult to speak, hear or drive, and this is why men rarely talk much during sex. Sometimes a woman needs to listen to his breathing to monitor his progress. Men love to hear women talk 'dirty' about what she can and will do for him – but only *before* sex, not during. A man may experience a loss of direction (and erection) when a woman talks to him during sex. During sex, a man uses his right brain, and brain scans show that he's so intent on what he is doing, he's virtually deaf.

For a man to talk during sex, he needs

to switch to his left brain. A woman

can multi-track sex and speech.

For a woman, talk is a crucial part of foreplay because words are all-important to her. If during sex, a man stops talking, a woman may think he isn't interested in her. A man needs to practise lots of love talk during foreplay to fulfil a woman's needs. A woman, however, needs to stop talking during sex, and just use vocal sounds to keep a man interested – lots of 'oooh's' and 'aaahs' give a man the positive feedback he needs to achieve fulfilment. If a woman talks during sex, a man feels obliged to respond and the moment can be lost.

A woman's brain is not pre-wired to respond to the chemicals of sex drive as dramatically as a man's brain. During sex, a woman is acutely aware of outside sounds or environmental changes, but a man will be totally focused and undistracted. This is a woman's ancient nest-defending biology in action – she is monitoring sounds to make sure nothing is sneaking up to steal her offspring. As many men have found, trying to entice a woman to make love in an open area, or in a room with thin walls or unlocked doors can be a great way to start an argument. It also throws light on why this inbuilt fear is most women's secret fantasy – having sex in a public place.

The Orgasm Objective

'She just uses me whenever she wants and then forgets about me. I hate being a sex object!' These words have *never* been uttered by any man. A man's criterion for fulfilment is orgasm and he mistakenly assumes that it is also a woman's. 'How could she possibly feel fulfilled without orgasm?' he wonders. A man can't imagine such a situation for himself and so he uses a woman's orgasm as the measure of his own success as a lover. This expectation puts enormous pressure on women to perform and actually reduces their chances of orgasm. A woman needs the feelings of closeness and warmth and the build-up of tension for great sex, and she usually sees orgasm as an extra – not the objective. A man always needs orgasm, but a woman does not. Men see women as their sexual mirrors and spend ages pumping and thrusting away, thinking that's what she really wants. Look at the next chart and study the peaks and troughs of a woman's sex drive throughout the year. The peaks are when she is most likely to want an orgasm – around the time of ovulation – and the troughs are where she needs lots of cuddles and non-sexual touching. You will notice that a woman's desire for sex is highest in the autumn. This means more babies will be born in the summer giving them a greater chance of survival due to warmer temperatures and more plentiful food.

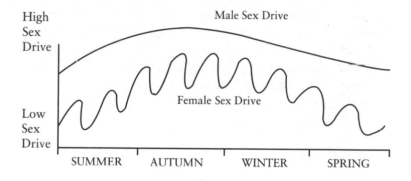

Male and female sex drives

A common fantasy for most men is a sensuous, unknown woman coming on to him and finding him irresistible. He satisfies her every need – *her* every need. A man's measurement of his prowess as a lover is directly related to *her* level of satisfaction and so he constantly monitors her reactions to see how well he's doing.

Men don't fake orgasm – no man wants

to pull a face like that on purpose.

Most men do not have the ability to sense a woman's intimate feelings and emotions during sex which is another reason why her orgasm is so important to him. It proves to him he must have done a good job, he achieved a result. Most men never understand that compulsory orgasm is a man's criterion for success; it's not necessarily a woman's. For a woman, an orgasm is an added bonus, not a measurement.

What Turns Us On?

Here is a list of the top turn-ons for both sexes, showing how men and women do not understand each others' sexual needs. The list of preferences is a direct reflection of the brainset of men and women. Men are visual and want sex. Women are auditory and feeling and want touch and romance.

Women's Turn-Ons	Men's Turn-Ons
1. Romance	1. Pornography
2. Commitment	2. Female nudity
3. Communication	3. Sexual variety
4. Intimacy	4. Lingerie
5. Non-sexual touching	5. Her availability

A man's biological job is to find as many healthy females as possible and help them conceive. A woman's biological role is to bear children and find a partner who will stick around long enough to raise them. For both, these ancient forces are driving them on, despite living in an age in which procreation for survival is no longer relevant. This is why commitment is such a turn-on for women, with romance containing the subtle promise of a man's readiness to help raise the offspring. This is why women need monogamy, and we'll discuss this in the next chapter.

For a woman to criticise a man's need for visual stimulation is like a man criticising a woman for wanting to talk or go out to dinner. The answer is to have both.

How Men Get a Raw Deal

The things that turn men on are often described as dirty, disgusting, crude or perverted, particularly by women. Overall, women are not aroused by the items on a man's turn-on list and men show little reaction to the items on a woman's list.

The public generally glorifies women's turn-ons in movies, books and advertisements, and condemns men's as pornographic or crude. From a biological standpoint, however, each needs these factors to feel aroused. Public criticism of men's turn-ons is what drives men to hide their *Playboy* magazines and deny they have secret fantasies. Many men's needs remain unfulfilled and many feel guilt or resentment. When a man and a woman understand the history and evolution of their desires, it makes it easier to understand and accept, without anger, resentment or guilt. No person should do anything they do not feel comfortable with but having an open discussion about each others' needs can help to enhance a more loving relationship. A man also needs to understand that it takes less effort for him to organise a romantic dinner or weekend away than it is for a woman to dress in suspenders and swing from a chandelier.

The Aphrodisiac Myth

Of the hundreds of popularised aphrodisiacs around, none have been scientifically shown to work. They work on what is called the placebo effect – if you think it will work, it probably will. Some so-called aphrodisiacs can even help inhibit or constrain sexual desire, particularly when they irritate the kidneys, and cause itching and rashes. The only aphrodisiacs guaranteed to work are those on the list of what turns us on.

Men and Their Pornography

Men love pornography and women don't. For men, it appeals to their biological urges by showing clear images of shapes, lust and sex, but many women see it as showing the domination of women by insensitive men. There has been no evidence to prove a connection between pornography and sex crimes. It can, however, be psychologically damaging to men and women simply because it shows men hung like donkeys who can keep thrusting mindlessly for hours. This can significantly affect the expectations a man has about his own performance.

What's the difference between

erotic and kinky?

Erotic is when you use a feather.

Kinky is when you use the whole chicken.

Pornography also implies that women have the same visual and physical arousal criteria as men, and that a woman's sex drive is as strong as or higher than a man's. It can have a detrimental impact on women too. Showing them being treated as sex objects and having a totally unrealistic hunger for physical sex can damage a woman's self-esteem.

But while surveys of 18–23 year olds show that 50% of men feel that their sex life is not as good as that portrayed in movies, TV and magazines, 62% of women feel their sex life is as good as or better than media depictions. It appears that men are more affected by their performance expectations than women.

Are There Female Sex Maniacs?

If aliens from outer space landed on Earth and surveyed a selection of our men's and women's magazines, books and movies, they would quickly reach the conclusion that human females are a highly sexed lot who are all multi-orgasmic and just can't get enough. If the aliens then read or watched the kind of pornography we routinely produce, they would be convinced that women have an insatiable sexual appetite and will bonk almost any man under nearly any circumstances. This is the image that modern women have been expected to live up to by the media. In reality, the voracious female sex maniac is a figment of most men's imaginations and accounts for less than one percent of all women. A modern woman now has difficulty believing a man who tells her that he likes the way she looks when she's naked. This fantasy image usually only affects modern men and women because their parents and grandparents were never exposed to this idea of a woman possessing a man's sex drive. Many women, however, feel abnormal or even frigid because they don't measure up to these media images. Men have been coaxed into believing that women now have high sex drives and this makes men feel angry or frustrated when women don't initiate sex often enough. With magazine article headlines like, 'Become multi-orgasmic in five days!', 'How to bed a European Lover', 'Tantric Sex – keep it going for hours', 'I had 300 lovers in three

years!' and 'How to keep him hard all night', it's no wonder that men and women are befuddled into thinking that
women have only sex on their minds.

> *The women's movement freed*
>
> *modern women's attitudes to*
>
> *their sexuality, but it did not*
>
> *increase their basic urge to have sex.*

Women's sex drive has probably remained the same for
thousands of years and all that has changed is that it is now
open for discussion. The sex drive of a modern woman is
probably no different to that of her mother or grandmoth-
er, but the older generation of women suppressed it and
certainly didn't discuss it. Before the Pill arrived, sexual
frustration must have been a good deal higher. But certainly not as high as the media today would have us believe.

Lights Off or On?

As we now know, men are visual when it comes to sex.
They want to see shapes, curves, nudes, pornography.
Kinsey found that 76% of men said they wanted sex with
the lights on, compared to only 36% of women. Overall,
women are not stimulated by nudity unless it is a nude couple in a romantic or suggestive scene. When a man sees a
woman naked he becomes highly stimulated and aroused.
When a woman sees a man naked, she usually bursts into
laughter.

Women love words and feelings. They prefer sex with
the lights down or off or with their eyes closed, as this

perfectly suits a woman's finely tuned sensory equipment. Gentle stroking, sensual touches and whispering sweet nothings will turn on most women. Nude male centrefolds come and go as women's magazines try to persuade us that women's attitudes to nudity are now the same as men's. These centrefolds vanish just as quickly as they appear, but it has been shown that they increase overall readership by gay men.

> *Most women prefer sex with the*
>
> *lights out – they can't bear to see*
>
> *a man enjoying himself.*
>
> *Men like sex with the lights on –*
>
> *so they can get the woman's name right.*

All attempts at selling porn to women have failed although, during the late 1990s, there was an increase in the sale of semi-naked male pin-up calendars, which ended up outstripping the sales of female nude calendars. The buyers of nude male calenders have been shown to fall into three categories – teenage girls who want pictures of their favourite movie or rock star, women who want it as a humorous joke for one of their friends, and gay men.

CHAPTER 10
MARRIAGE, LOVE AND ROMANCE

'...I want openness, honesty, and a monogamous relationship. I'm not into men who want to play games!'

Pair-bonding, that is, one man–one woman, has been the general living concept for humans for a long time. It was usually an arrangement where a male kept his favourite female and, if he could afford to feed them, several other females, plus a range of indiscriminate sexual encounters on the side.

Modern marriage was an invention of Judeo–Christian ideals and was a subtle form of recruitment. By convincing two adults to commit to a set of rules demanding obedience to a God, the offspring of the marriage would automatically be born into the parents' religion. Whenever any human activity, however, is surrounded by elaborate rituals and public declarations, it is usually contrary to our biology and is intended to make people do something they would not naturally do. Peach-faced birds do not need an elaborate ceremony for them to 'marry' – it is their natural biological state. To insist that a polygamous animal like a ram agrees to a contract of marriage to a single ewe is equally ridiculous. This is not to say that marriage has no place in modern society. We, the authors, are married, but it's important to understand its history and its relation to our biology.

Marriage has its good side. It teaches you loyalty, forbearance, tolerance, self-restraint, and other valuable qualities you wouldn't need if you stayed single.

So, what's the advantage of marriage to men? In basic evolutionary terms, nothing. A man is like a rooster whose urge is to spread his genetic seed as widely as possible and as often as he can. Yet the majority of men still marry, and divorced men remarry or live in pseudo-married states. This shows society's remarkable ability to restrain biologically promiscuous men.

Sex is the price women pay for marriage.

Marriage is the price men pay for sex.

When asked, 'What can marriage offer you?', most men will mumble something about having a warm safe refuge, having their food cooked for them, their clothes ironed. At base, they want a cross between their mother and a personal servant. Psychoanalyst Sigmund Freud said such men probably have a mother/son relationship with their wives. Only 22% of men mention their female partner as their best friend. The best friend of most men is usually another man, because they understand each other's thought processes. When asked, 'Who's your best friend?' 86% of women said it was another woman, in other words, someone with similar brain-wiring.

When men walk down the aisle, many see it as the beginning of an endless supply of sex-on-demand, but this expectation, never discussed *before* marriage, is not how women see it. Surveys do reveal, however, that married men have more sex than single men, with married men aged between 25 and 50 averaging three times a week, whereas only half the single men have that much. The single man's average is less than once a week. In 1999 in Australia 20% of single men did not have sex in the year of the survey and three per cent of married men also missed out. As we've already discussed, sex is marvellous for overall health. Unmarried or widowed men also have a higher premature death rate than married men.

Why Women Need Monogamy

Even though marriage in Western societies has become a toothless tiger from a legal standpoint, it is still the ambition of most women and 91% of people still get married. This is because, for a woman, marriage is a declaration to the world that a man regards her as 'special' and intends to have a monogamous relationship with her. This feeling of being 'special' has a dramatic effect on the chemical action in a woman's brain which is evidenced by research showing that a woman's orgasm rate is four to five times higher in a marital bed and two to three times higher in a monogamous relationship.

There is a feeling among older people that the young think marriage is an outdated institution. A survey in 1998 of 2,344 male and female college students aged 18–23, equally divided between the sexes, found this not to be the case. When asked about commitment, 84% of women, compared to 70% of men, said they would marry some day. Only 5% of men and 2% of women felt marriage was obsolete.

Friendships were found to be more important than sexual relationships for 92% of both sexes. When it came to the notion of being married to one person for the rest of their lives, 86% of women liked the idea, compared to 75% of men. Only 35% of couples felt that today's relationships are better than those of their parents' generation. Fidelity was a high priority on women's lists, with 44% of the under–30s saying they would end a relationship if a man was unfaithful, a figure that dropped to 32% among women in their 30s. Of women in their 40s, 28% said they'd end it, while only 11% of women in their 60s felt the same. This all shows that the younger a woman is, the tougher she will be on a straying man, and the more important fidelity and monogamy are to her value system.

This is a difference that most men never understand. The majority believe having the odd fling will not affect their relationship because men have little problem separating sex from love in the brain. For women, however, sex and love are intertwined. A sexual liaison with another woman can be seen as the ultimate betrayal, and good reason for finishing a relationship.

If marriage fails as often as it does, why do so many of us keep doing it? Why not live on our own, or with our families or friends, and have lovers when the mood takes us? There are two answers. Firstly, happy stable marriages continue to be the most reliable way to bring up happy, healthy children. Secondly, marriage can have an enormous soothing effect. In a world where life is lived at breakneck speed, marriage at its best can function like a port in a storm, a place to rest and recuperate from the stresses which face us every day – a place to relax and be, both literally and psychologically, 'at home'.

Why Men Avoid Commitment

A man who is married or in a long-term relationship is always secretly worried that single men are having more sex and more fun. He imagines wild singles parties, adventurous, commitment-free coupling and jacuzzis full of naked supermodels. He fears opportunity is passing right by him, and he's missing out completely. It doesn't matter that, when he was single, such opportunities never presented themselves anyway. He forgets about those evenings sitting alone eating cold baked beans out of a can, the humiliating rebuffs from women in front of friends at parties and the long periods without sex. He just can't help worrying that commitment equals missing out.

Men want to wait for the perfect partner,

but all they usually get is older.

Where is Love in the Brain?

In June 2000, Professor Semin Zeki and Andrew Bartela at University College, London scanned the brains of 11 female and 6 male volunteers who all described themselves as 'madly in love' and had fallen in love within the past 6 to 12 months. They were shown alternating pictures of their lover plus pictures of friends of the same sex. The scientists found that seeing a lover activated 4 specific regions of the brain. Two areas lay in the cerebral cortex, the more advanced part of the brain. These were the medial insula, which is thought to be responsible for 'gut feelings' and part of the interior (cingulate), which is known to respond to euphoria-inducing drugs. Another two in the deeper and more primitive basal (ganglin) region of the brain were involved in finding experiences rewarding and play a role in addiction.

This research explains why when we are in love we are often in an euphoric, drug-like state and don't get depressed.

American anthropologist Dr Helen Fisher of Rutgers University, New Jersey, has also been carrying out pioneering work using brain scans in order to locate the position of love in the brain. While her research is still in the preliminary stages, she has located three types of emotion in the brain: lust, infatuation and attachment. Each emotion has its own specific brain chemistry which lights up the brain when its owner is attracted to someone. In biological terms, these three components of love have evolved to serve the vital function of ensuring reproduction. Once conception has occurred, the system deactivates itself and the love process stops.

The first stage, lust, is the physical and non-verbal attraction previously discussed. Fisher says, 'Infatuation is a stage where a person keeps popping into your brain and you can't get them out. Your brain focuses on the positive qualities of the sweetheart and ignores their bad habits.'

Infatuation is the brain's attempt to form a bond with a potential partner and it is an emotion so powerful that it can cause incredible euphoria. If someone is rejected it can also cause extraordinary despair and can lead to obsession. In extreme cases, it can even end in murder. At the infatuation stage, several powerful brain chemicals are released which cause feelings of elation. Dopamine gives the feeling of well-being, phenylethylamine increases excitement levels, serotonin creates a sense of emotional stability and norepinephrine induces the feeling that you can achieve anything. A sex addict is someone who becomes addicted to the hormonal cocktail of the infatuation stage and wants to stay permanently high. But infatuation is a temporary feeling lasting, on average, from 3 to 12 months, when most people mistakenly define it as love. It is, in fact, a biological trick by nature to guarantee that a man and a woman are thrown together long enough to procreate. The danger of this stage is that lovers believe their sex drives are perfectly matched, but only because they are going at it like rabbits. Their real sex drive differences reveal themselves only after the infatuation stage ends or the attachment stage begins.

*Infatuation is nature's biological
trick to guarantee that a man
and a woman are thrown
together long enough to procreate.*

When reality finally takes over from infatuation, either one or both of the partners will reject the other, or the third stage, attachment, will kick in, with its focus on building a co-operative bond that will last long enough to raise children. With more research and the rapid technological advancement in brain scanners, Fisher expects soon to have a formula for understanding the brain locations for love and emotions in both men and women. Understanding these three stages can make it easier to deal with the infatuation stage and to be prepared for its possible downside.

Love: Why Men Fall In and Women Fall Out

Love is said to be confusing, and this is especially true for men. Men are fuelled to the eyeballs with testosterone which leads them easily into the lust phase of falling in love. During the infatuation stage, men are so fired up on testosterone that most can't tell which way is up, down or sideways. Reality, when it hits home, can hit especially hard. The woman who was so exciting at midnight last night might not seem anywhere near as attractive next morning when the sun rises – and not all that intelligent either. But because the centres for emotion and reason are better connected in a woman's brain – and she's not out of control on testosterone – she finds it easier to evaluate whether a man is potentially the right partner for her. This is why most relationships are ended by women and why so many men are confused about what happened. Women are gentle in separation even when they are dumping a man. In a goodbye letter to him, some women will finish by drawing a happy face or saying they will always love him.

Why Men Can't Say 'I Love You'

Saying 'I love you' is never a problem for a woman. A woman's brain-wiring makes her world full of feelings, emotions, communication and words. A woman knows that when she feels warm, wanted and adored and is in the attachment stage, she's probably in love, but a man is not exactly sure what love is and he's likely to confuse lust and infatuation with love. All he knows is that he can't keep his hands off her so ... maybe that's love? His brain is blinded by testosterone, he has a constant erection and he can't think straight. It's often not until years after a relationship begins that a man recognises he was in love, but he does it in retrospect. Women recognise when love does not exist and that's why most relationships are ended by women.

Women recognise when love doesn't

exist. That's why they're much more

proactive in finishing relationships.

Many men are commitment-phobes. They are scared that saying the 'L' word commits them for the rest of their lives and spells the end of any chance of naked supermodels in jacuzzis. When a man eventually crosses the line by saying it, he then wants to tell everyone, everywhere. Most men, however, do not notice the increase in a woman's orgasm rate after he has said the 'L' word.

How Men Can Separate Love from Sex

The happily married woman who has an affair is rare, but the happily married male wanderer is common. More than 90% of affairs are initiated by men but more than 80% are ended by women. This is because when a woman begins to realise that the affair has no lasting emotional promise and will only be physical, she wants out. A man's brain, with its ability to separate love from sex and deal with each item separately because of its compartmentalisation, lets him see just one thing at a time. He's therefore often happy with just a good physical relationship – that's taken all his attention. It is still unclear exactly where love is situated in the brain, but research indicates that a woman's brain has a network of connections between her love centre and her sex centre (the hypothalamus), and the love centre needs to be activated before her sex centre can be switched on. Men do not appear to have these connections and so they can deal with sex or love separately. For a man, sex is sex and love is love, and sometimes they happen together.

The first question a woman will ask a man who has been caught having an affair is, 'Do you love the woman?' The man who answers, 'No, it was only physical, it didn't mean anything,' is likely to be telling the truth, because he can separate sex from love. A woman's brain is not wired to understand or accept this answer and this is why many women find it difficult to believe a man who says it meant nothing, because, for her, sex equals love. In a woman's mind, it is not the physical act of sex with the other woman that affects her as much as the violation of the emotional contract and trust she had in him. If a woman has an affair and says it didn't mean anything, she's probably lying. For a woman to cross the line to having sex, she would have already had to establish an emotional bond with the new man.

For women, love and sex are intertwined.

One equals the other.

When Women Make Love, Men Have Sex

An old adage holds that making love is what a woman does while a man is bonking her. What it actually is, however, often sparks arguments between lovers everywhere. A man will call sex 'sex' but a woman is likely to react negatively to the word as it is not, by her definition, the way it is. A woman 'makes love', meaning that she needs to feel loved and have loving feelings before she wants to have sex. To most women the act of 'sex' is generally seen as a loveless, gratuitous act because the wiring of a female brain does not identify with this definition.

When a man says 'sex', sometimes he means just physical sex, but this doesn't mean he doesn't love his woman. When a man wants to 'make love', he is still likely to call it 'sex'. This can have negative effects on a woman, but to use the expression 'make love' can make many men feel that they are being phoney or conning her, because sometimes he just wants sex. When a woman claims a man is 'sleeping' with someone, you can bet he is not sleeping. 'How could you sleep with her?' women ask. 'You don't even like her!' Emotionally, men and women do seem to inhabit different planets, but it's not necessarily down to a male lack of moral fibre. The bit of the brain that handles our emotions – the limbic system – has two parts. There is the old part (temporal limbic) which is the bit that deals with sex and violence, and a newer part (gyrus cinguli) which is more linked into thinking and imagining. Male brains are more active in the old part and are more tuned for action and women's brains are active in the newer part for 'symbolic emotional responses.' When men and women understand each other's perspective and agree not to judge each other's definition, this obstacle ceases to be a stumbling block in the relationship.

Why Great Partners Look Attractive

Studies at the Kinsey Institute reveal that during love-making a man's perception of his woman is related to the depth of his intimate feelings for her. This means that he rates her higher on the physical attractiveness scale if he's madly in love with her, even if others feel that, when she's naked, she'd look more like the Michelin Man. He rates her lower in attractiveness if he does not particularly care for her, even though she may be physically stunning. When a man is turned on by a woman, the size of her thighs becomes irrelevant. In fact, they're perfect. This demonstrates that while a woman's physical attractiveness rates highly in initial meetings for men, a warm nurturing partnership accounts for a significant part of her attractiveness in the long-term and this is confirmed by the surveys of 'what we look for' in Chapter 9. This is not the case with a man's attractiveness to a woman, however. This has been illuminated by some interesting studies carried out in singles bars. Researchers found that the later the hour, the more attractive the available women looked to the unattached men. A woman who was rated by the men as a five out of ten at 7pm, was rated seven by 10.30pm, and eight-and-a-half at midnight, with alcohol levels enhancing the scores. With women, however, a man who rated a five at 7pm was still given the same mark at midnight.

For a woman, a man who rates a five at 7pm still rates the same score at midnight, regardless of how much she's had to drink.

Alcohol did not increase his attractiveness rating and, in some cases, it even decreased his rating. Women still evaluate a man's viability as a partner by his personal characteristics above his physical appearance, regardless of the hour or the amount of alcohol consumed. Men increase a woman's attractiveness rating relative to the odds that she will let him carry out his role as a professional sperm donor.

Do Opposites Attract?

Groundbreaking studies by scientists in 1962 found we are drawn to people with similar values, interests, attitudes and perceptions, and these are people with whom we instantly 'click'. Subsequent studies showed that lovers have a greater chance of a long-term relationship under these conditions. Too many similarities, however, can also become boring. We need just enough difference to make it interesting and to complement our own personalities, yet not so much that it will interfere with our lifestyles. A quiet man, for example, might be attracted to an outgoing woman and a woman who is a worrier may zero in on a relaxed, laid-back partner.

Physical Opposites Attract

Look at any study or survey of what attracts us physically to the opposite sex and you'll find that we prefer opposite physical features to our own. Men prefer women with softness and curves where men have firmness and flat areas. Men prefer women with wide hips, narrow waists, long legs and round chests – all attributes they will never possess. He prefers smaller chins and noses and a flat stomach, too, as he will normally have the opposite.

Women also prefer the opposite in men, including wider shoulders, narrower hips, thicker legs and arms, stronger chins and fuller noses. Yet there are some interesting exceptions. Some studies, for example, have found that men who don't drink alcohol prefer women with small breasts, women with large breasts prefer men with small noses, and men with large noses usually hang out with flat-chested women. Extroverted men prefer women with very large breasts.

The Hips-to-Waist Ratio is the Key

If you look at men's tastes over the centuries you will see that they have gone ga-ga over everything from large, fleshy 16th Century models to the pencil-skinny supermodels who look more like asparagus spears. The one thing that has remained constant, however, is a woman's hip-to-waist ratio which never fails to grab a man's attention. Women with a hip-to-waist measurement of 70% waist size relative to hips have been shown to have a higher fertility rate and better health than other women. Dr Devendra Singh of Cambridge University surveyed men of many nationalities to find that men had unconsciously learned to read this information somewhere in their past, and now have it pre-wired into their brains.

The good news for women is that if your waist measurement is between 67% to 80% that of your hips, you'll get men's attention even if you are 5 to 10 kilos overweight as the curves are the essential criteria. As a bonus, women with these ratios are also perceived by men as humorous, sexy, healthy and intelligent. Women with a higher ratio, that is, thick waist, are seen as caring and faithful. Women who are too thin are perceived as ambitious and aggressive.

Women everywhere prefer a

small, tight rear on a man,

although few women know why.

Women still go for the V-shaped man with broad shoulders, narrow waist and strong arms, which were all the original prerequisites of the successful lunch-chaser. A strong chin, nose and brow also appeal because they give a man a greater chance of surviving a heavy blow to the front of the head. Women everywhere also prefer a small tight rear on a man, although few will have any idea why they find that so attractive. We are the only primate that has a protruding rear and its purpose is two-fold. Firstly, it helps us stand upright. And secondly, it ensures that a man can give a strong forward thrust during sex to increase the chance of fertilisation.

Men and Romance

It's not that men don't want to romance women, it's just that they don't understand its importance to women. The books we buy are a clear indicator of the things that interest us. Women spend millions every year on romantic novels. Women's magazines concentrate on love, romance, other people's affairs or how to exercise, eat and dress better to have even more romance. One Australian study showed that women who read romance novels have sex twice as often as those who don't. Conversely, men spend millions on books and magazines teaching technical know-how on a range of spatially-related subjects, from computers and mechanical apparatus to lunch-chasing activities like fishing, hunting and football.

It's no wonder when it comes to romance that most men generally don't know what to do. This is understandable as a modern man has never had a role model. His father didn't know what to do either, as it was never an issue for him. A woman at one of our conferences recently said that she had asked her husband to show her more affection – so he washed and polished her car. This demonstrates how men see 'doing things' as a way of showing they care. The same husband bought her a car jack for her birthday and got her front row seats at a wrestling match for their tenth wedding anniversary.

Never forget that a woman is a romantic. She enjoys wine, flowers, and chocolate. Let her know that you, too, remember these things ... by speaking of them occasionally.

Woody Allen

While European men have a somewhat over-exaggerated reputation for romance, the vast majority of men, in every corner of the world, haven't got a clue. Previous generations of men were too busy making ends meet to have to worry about such finesse. Besides, men's brains are wired for the technical and not the aesthetic. It's not that a man won't try, he just doesn't understand the significance of opening a car door, sending flowers, dancing, cooking for a woman, or changing a toilet roll. A woman enters a new relationship looking for romance and love. Sex comes as a consequence. Men frequently enter a relationship through sex and then look to see if there could be the possibility of a relationship.

Some Surefire Romance Tips for Men

Women don't have a problem when it comes to love and romance, but most men are in the dark about it so they simply make sure they're ready for love any time, any place. A man's romantic skills (or lack thereof) play a significant part in whether a woman will feel like having sex with him, so here are six tried and tested things that work as well for men today as they did 5,000 years ago.

How do you know if a man is

ready for sex? He's breathing.

1. **Set the environment.** When you consider a woman's sensitivity to her surroundings and the high receptivity of her senses to outside stimuli, it makes sense that a man pays attention to the environment. Women's oestrogen hormones make her sensitive to the right lighting – dimly-lit rooms make pupils dilate, so people look attractive to each other and skin blemishes and wrinkles are less noticeable. A woman's superior hearing means the right music is important, and a clean, secure cave is

better than one that can be invaded by children or other people at any moment. Women's insistence on sex in private explains why most women's private fantasy is of having sex in public, while a man's private fantasy is sex with a stranger.

2. **Feed her.** Having evolved as a lunch-chaser, you'd think it would occur to a man that providing a woman with food stirs up primal female feelings. This is why taking a woman to dinner is a significant event for her even when she's not hungry because the provision of food shows his attention to her well-being and survival. Cooking a meal for a woman has an even deeper intrinsic meaning as it brings out primitive feelings in both a man and a woman.

3. **Light a fire.** Collecting wood and lighting a fire to give warmth and protection has been done by men for women for hundreds of thousands of years, and appeals to most women's romantic side. Even if it's a gas fire that she can light easily herself, he needs to light it if he wants to set a romantic atmosphere. The pay-off comes from the act of providing for her needs, not from the fire itself.

4. **Bring flowers.** Most men do not understand the power of a bunch of fresh flowers. Men think, 'Why spend so much money on something that will be dead and thrown out in a few days?' It makes sense to a man's logical mind to give a woman a pot plant because, with constant care and attention, it will survive – in fact, you could even make a profit on it! However, a woman doesn't see it that way – she wants a fresh bunch of flowers. After a few days the flowers die and are thrown out, but this presents an opportunity for him to buy another bunch and once again bring out her romantic side by providing for her needs.

5. **Go dancing.** It's not that men don't want to dance, it's

just that many of them don't have the location in the right brain required to feel rhythm. Go to any aerobics class and watch the male participants (if any turn up) trying to keep time. When a man takes dancing lessons for basic rock 'n' roll and waltz, he will be the hit of the party with *all* women. Dancing has been described as a vertical act of horizontal desire and that's its history – it's a ritual that evolved to allow close male/female body contact as a lead-up to courtship, just as it did with other animals.

6. **Buy chocolates and champagne.** This combination has long been associated with romance, although few people know why. Champagne contains a chemical not found in other alcoholic beverages which increases testosterone levels. Chocolate contains phenylethylamine which stimulates a woman's love centre in the brain. Recent research by Danielle Piomella at the Neurosciences Institute in San Diego discovered three new chemicals called N-acylethanolamines, which attach themselves to the cannabis receptors in a woman's brain, giving her sensations similar to being high on marijuana. These chemicals are in brown chocolate and cocoa, but not in white chocolate or coffee.

Why Men Stop Touching and Talking

'Before we were married he would hold my hand in public, rub my back and talk endlessly to me. Now he never holds my hand and doesn't want to talk – and he only touches me when he wants sex.' Does this complaint sound familiar?

After marriage a man knows all he needs to know about his partner and sees no point in excessive talk.

During courtship, a man touches his girlfriend more than at any other time in their relationship. This is because he is dying to 'get his hands on her', but he hasn't received the green light for any sexual touching so he touches her everywhere else instead. When he gets the go-ahead for sexual touching, his brain sees no point in going back to 'the old days'. So he just concentrates on the 'good bits'. He talks a lot during courtship to collect information – facts and data about his girlfriend – and to give her information about himself. By the time they're married, he knows all he needs to know about her and sees little point in excessive talk. But when a man understands that a woman's brain is programmed to communicate with talk and that her sensitivity to touch is ten times greater than his, he can teach himself to become skillful in these areas and the overall quality of his love life will dramatically improve.

Why Men Grope and Women Don't

The hormone oxytocin is known as the 'cuddle hormone', and it's released when someone's skin is gently stroked or they are cuddled. It increases sensitivity to touch and the feelings of bonding, and is a major factor in a woman's behaviour towards babies and men. When a woman begins breast-feeding it triggers the 'let down' reflex that releases milk from the breasts.

If a woman wants to pleasure a man by touching him, she normally does it the way she would like to receive it.

She scratches his head, caresses his face, rubs his back and tenderly brushes his hair. This type of touch has little impact on most men and can even be annoying. His skin is significantly less sensitive to touch than a woman's in order that he won't feel pain or injury during the hunt. Men prefer to be touched in mainly one area, and as often as possible. This creates major relationship problems. When a man decides to sensually touch a woman, he gives her the things he likes – he gropes her breasts and crotch. This is at the top of a woman's hate list and causes resentment on both sides. When a man and woman learn to give each other sensual touch based on their individual needs and skin sensitivity, their relationship is even more enriched.

Is There Love in Springtime?

Nature's biological clock works to allow female animals to give birth in the warm part of the year to ensure survival of the offspring. If it takes a species, say, three months to give birth, nature makes the males randiest in the spring so the young are born in summer. For humans, gestation takes nine months and so a man's testosterone level is highest nine months earlier, in the autumn. The old adage, 'In the Spring a man's fancy turns to love' only applies to species that have a short gestation period of about three months.

'Love in the spring' is only for animals

who bear offspring quickly.

Research shows that in the Southern Hemisphere a man's testosterone is highest in March and, in the Northern Hemisphere, in September. Men have also been shown to be more competent at map-reading during these months because spatial ability is enhanced by testosterone. (Turn back to the chart in Chapter 9 and you'll see how this happens.)

How to Think Sexy

Because the mind is a cocktail of chemical reactions, it is possible to think yourself into feeling sexy. This technique is taught by many sex therapists. It involves concentrating only on the positive aspects of your partner and recalling exciting sexual experiences you've had together. The brain reacts by bringing into play the chemicals that drive your sex urge and make you feel sexual. This reaction is obvious during the infatuation stage or courtship when a lover can see only good in their sweetheart and their sex drives seem endless. It is also possible to think yourself out of sex by concentrating on a partner's negatives, which prevents the brain from releasing the chemicals necessary for a sex drive.

Recreating Infatuation

The good news is that because you can think yourself into sex, you can also think yourself into infatuation whenever you want by recreating the courtship routines that existed early in your relationship. This is why candlelit dinners, romantic beach walks and weekends away together work so well, by giving couples a hormonal 'hit' – the feeling that has often been described as a 'natural high' and 'high on love'. Lovers who expect the exhilaration of infatuation to last forever are sadly disappointed but, with effective planning, it can be recreated whenever you feel the need.

How to Find the Right Partner

Love starts with lust which can last a few hours, a few days or a few weeks. Next comes infatuation which lasts, on average, 3 to 12 months before attachment takes over. When the blinding cocktail of hormones subsides after a year or so, we now see our partner in the cold light of day and those little habits we found so endearing at first begin to become irritating. Once you thought it was cute that he could never find things in the fridge, but now it makes you want to scream. He used to love hearing you talk about every little thing but now he's contemplating murder. You silently ask yourself, 'Can I live like this for the rest of my life? What do we have in common?'

The flower of love is the rose. After three days all the petals fall off and you're left with an ugly, prickly thing.

Chances are you don't have much in common or much to talk about. Nature's objective is to throw men and women together under the influence of a powerful hormonal cocktail that causes them to procreate and *not* think. Finding the right partner means deciding what things you will have in common with someone *in the long-term*, and to do this in advance of nature's blinding hormonal highs. When infatuation has passed – and pass it will – can you maintain a lasting relationship based on friendship and common interests? Write a list of the traits and interests you want in a long-term partner and then you'll know *exactly* who you are looking for. A man will have a list of qualities for his ideal mate but when he goes to a party, his brain is fired up by testosterone. It then searches for the 'ideal' woman based on hormonal motivation – nice legs, flat stomach, round bum, good breasts, and so on, all features connected with short-term procreation. Women want a man who is sensitive and caring, has a V-shaped torso and a great personality, all things connected to child-rearing, lunch-chasing and protecting. These are also short-term biological needs and have little to do with success in a modern relationship. When you write a list of the desirable long-term characteristics in your perfect partner and keep it handy, it helps you to be objective about a new person the next time nature tries to control your thoughts and urges.

Nature wants you to procreate as often as possible and it uses powerful drugs to push you into it. When you understand this and are armed with a job description of your ideal long-term mate, you are less likely to be tricked and more likely to be successful in your hunt for that elusive perfect partner with whom you'll be finally able to live happily ever after.

CHAPTER 11
TOWARDS A
DIFFERENT FUTURE

'We may never know what motivated our
fish ancestors to come out of the water.'
David Attenborough, naturalist

They say it's great to be a man because you can walk topless on the beach in Tunisia without getting stoned to death, you don't have to remember where you left things, you can open your own jars and eat a banana in front of builders. It's great to be a woman because you can buy your own clothes, cross your legs without adjusting yourself and if you slap a man's face in public, everyone thinks you're in the right.

It's great to be a man because you

can buy cucumbers and marrows

without getting embarrassed.

Men and women are different. Not better or worse – but different. Science knows it, but political correctness does everything it can to deny it. There is a social and political view that men and women should be treated equally, based on the strange belief that men and women are the same. They are demonstrably not.

What Do Men and Women Really Want?

For modern men, not much has changed over the centuries. Eighty-seven percent of men today say their work is the most important thing in their life and 99% say they want a great sex life. For modern women, however, many of their priorities are quite different to those of their mothers and grandmothers.

Many women have chosen professional careers because they want some of the things men have: money, prestige and power. Studies now show that career women are also getting many of the other male side-effects: heart problems, ulcers, stress and premature death.

More than one in three women takes nine days off each year due to stress.

Forty-four percent of career women say their work is now their greatest source of stress. A survey of 5,000 women conducted by the British private health insurance company BUPA and health magazine *Top Santé* showed that 66% felt overwork was damaging their health.

Most women also said that if money was no object, they would prefer to be a homemaker or 'lady of leisure' and only 19% said they were interested in actually being a career woman. In a similar survey in Australia, careers only rated a top priority for five percent of women aged 18–65 and motherhood ranked as the number one choice across the board. Sixty percent of women in the 31–39 age group said that motherhood was their first choice, as compared with 2% for careers. For 31% of women aged 18–30 motherhood was also number one and careers accounted for only 18%.

Across the board, 80% of all women put raising their children in traditional families at the top of their priority list, showing that media hype and the feminist drive have not had as big an impact on women's attitudes as has been previously believed. The values and priorities of modern women are basically the same as they have been for centuries. The dramatic difference is that 93% of modern women say financial independence is vital to them and 62% want more power in politics – in other words they don't want to be dependent on men.

As for their personal lives, sex rated as the top priority for a mere 1% of women, compared to 45% for trust and 22% for respect. Only 20% of women said their sex life was fantastic, and 63% said their partner was not a wonderful lover. The bottom line is that motherhood still rates top of most women's list of things that give the greatest satisfaction. Many career women say they work for the money and most of these live in cities where two incomes are critical for survival. Many seem to believe that earning money to feed, clothe and educate the next generation is a more noble cause than rearing it. Women enjoy parenting more than men and, unfortunately, most men never get to appreciate it until they are grandparents.

Occupational Choices

Overall, occupational choices haven't changed much for men with spatially-related careers still being their number one choice. There has been a increase in the number of men entering traditionally female jobs, but a study of these men would show they have, to a greater or lesser extent, female-wired brains. This is obvious in areas such as hairdressing and creative arts, and less obvious in counselling and teaching.

For women, however, some things have changed, with 84% of working women in the USA now being part of the information and service sectors. In the Western world, between half and two-thirds of all new businesses are owned by women, and they now hold over 40% of executive, administration and management posts.

If you are a woman working in a traditional male hierarchy, you have two choices: quit or masculinise.

In traditional male hierarchies, women still have to struggle to get the top jobs but, as we've seen, most women don't want these positions anyway. In most political systems, less than five percent of politicians are female although they seem to attract 50% of the media coverage. If you are a woman working in a traditional male hierarchy, you have one of two choices for success; one is to quit and get a job where women receive a fair go, the other is to behave more like a man. Maleness still opens doors, and studies confirm that women who wear more 'masculine' clothes have a better chance of being selected for management positions than those dressed in 'feminine' styles – even when the decision-maker is a woman. Male interviewers also have a preference for candidates who are not wearing perfume.

The Feminising of Business

Male characteristics and values are largely responsible for driving people to the top of the tree but feminine values are fast becoming the only way to stay there.

Traditionally, most organisations have been controlled by a male hierarchy with a dominant male leader whose credo was, 'Follow me – or else!' These organisations are today rapidly becoming rarities, just as the school tough guy, who rose to the top at a time when brawn was respected over brains, is now also roundly despised. Masculine priorities need to be understood by any person aiming for the top of the heap, but feminine value systems are now much better suited to making the whole show work more efficiently, harmoniously and, therefore, successfully.

At the top levels, an emphasis on masculine values leads to internal power struggles. Individuals want to 'go it alone' when agreement cannot be reached. Initiative and intuitive hunches have no place in the fight to look, and be, the best, regardless of whether new strategies or lateral approaches might encourage new growth and development. Feminine values, on the other hand, encourage teamwork, collaboration and interdependence which are far better suited to an organisation's strategic capabilities and human resources. This doesn't mean that a man needs to be effeminate or a woman needs to be masculine, but men and women need to understand that each gender system is vital at different times in the rise to the top.

What to Do About Boys

Boys everywhere are failing at school so they need different schooling to girls. Between 80%–90% of expulsions in schools in the Western world are boys. Almost all-hyperactive children are boys and this condition is rarely seen in girls. Instead of dropping subjects that don't appeal to their mindset (which is what girls do) boys drop out of school and become responsible for most community crime. While girls are praised for their ability to compose and send emails to each other on the computer, boys are suspended for their ability to crack school computer codes and locate X-rated pictures on the Internet. Overall, boys are doing poorly in many areas of schoolwork. Male role-models have deserted the teaching profession and in primary schools women now dominate teaching and the few men who remain have traded their suits and ties for woolly cardigans.

Competition has been replaced by co-operation, learning facts replaced by empathising with world suffering, and bossy teachers retrained to become gentle facilitators – it's all become very caring and sharing. Out with discipline, in with niceness. Boys are left in a void with no-one to role-model maleness.

One answer is to have single-sex schools or single-sex classes and to encourage masculine role models back into teaching. We are not suggesting a return to the old days of bullying or the cane – boys need to be taught the value of respect, tolerance and co-operation – but they also need to be shown authority, discipline, competition and masculine role-modelling. The feminising of education has divided boys into two groups – the soft, gentle types and the undisciplined bullies and school dropouts.

No Role Models For Boys

Role models for girls are plentiful with most women still role-modelling warmth, communication and nurturing to the younger female generation. While female role models such as Elle MacPherson, Barbra Streisand, Hillary Clinton, the late Princess Diana and Madonna all showed masculine attributes like self assertiveness and sexual independence, they also role-modelled the typical female nurturing behaviours. Even the Iron Lady, Margaret Thatcher, had no problem with showing her feminine side in the face of human tragedy or loss. But boys now lack male role-models. Past male role-models included Clarke Gable, James Dean and James Bond who all displayed classic male traits but they also role-modelled manners, courtesy, respect for women and would defend their family or friends if necessary. These role-models have been replaced by Sylvester Stalone, Arnold Schwarzenegger, Bruce Willis and

Jean Claude Van Damme playing characters who use violence to solve their problems and cause mindless destruction of other people's property; or wimpy characters like Hugh Grant who role-models more female behaviours than male. Four out of five primary school teachers are now female and more and more boys are being raised by single mothers. A man who role-models a traditional male attribute such as holding a door open for a woman can be accused of being sexist, chauvinist or aggressive.

The Sports Hero

Many boys no longer have an older male role-model in their lives and this has paved the way for a new role model – the sports hero. For nearly 200 years the objectives of sport were twofold; first, to allow young men to burn up their testosterone, which benefited the entire community and second, to teach the life skills and values that help young people to become effective adults. The importance of ethics and fairness, being a good team player, and the principles of achieving personal and team goals were passed on to younger generations. Players were taught consideration and respect of other participants and the players were considered to be more important than the game. Since the 1980s, however, most sporting activities have become controlled by money and players regularly receive staggering amounts of money for their spatial ability – hitting, kicking or throwing something at a target. In most sports today, the game has become more important than the players. Where else can you now see greater displays of temper, violence, aggression, egotism and contempt for others than on a sports field? In past generations sport was used for character development and the player's well-being was paramount because money was never an issue. Today, players are left on the field crumpled, abused, broken, demoralised or half-dead as the pack pushes the ball over the line and everyone gets paid. In the clubs and hotels after the game, young men are shown the role-modelling of crude behaviour, severe drunkenness and general disrespect for others. Assaults on umpires or even biting off an opponent's ear are considered humorous by some fans.

The phenomena of the sports hero has brought some ominous role-modelling to the youth of sports-crazy nations. Like pop stars, they can be an unknown one day and revered as gods the next, often giving half-baked, inexperienced advice to impressionable young people.

Sports heroes are used to sell almost every type of merchandise and product imaginable. Many people in society, particularly young men, now believe that their measure of worth as an individual is related to how well they can kick a ball or hit a target.

The sports hero syndrome is not as big a problem in Europe where, mainly due to colder climate, indoor activities or cultural pursuits are encouraged. As a result, Beethoven is as well known in Europe as Michael Jordan or David Beckham.

Is This All Politically Correct?

We surveyed more than 10,000 conference delegates in six countries where political correctness is high on the political agenda, and found that 98% of men and 94% of women felt it had become an oppressive concept that stifled their freedom to say what they felt without censure.

Political correctness, in regard to gender, was originally intended to combat sexist attitudes, language, male/female inequalities and to give women equal opportunity. Women were supposedly being oppressed by dominant men, but, clearly, political correctness is not supported by the majority. So, will it ever work? Scientists say that it's unlikely. It has taken a million years for men and women to evolve into what they are today, and it will probably take another million years for them to evolve into beings that match a politically correct environment. The biggest problem humankind faces today is that their lofty ideals and concepts of behaviour are a million years ahead of their genetic reality.

Our Biology Hasn't Changed Much

Boys want to play with things; girls want to interact with people. Boys want to control, dominate and reach the top, but girls are more concerned with morality, relationships and people. Women are still a minority in big business and the political arena, but not because of male oppression. It's just that women are not interested in those things.

Despite the best intentions of equal opportunity employers, boys still stubbornly go into jobs with a mechanical and spatial bias and girls seem compelled to seek jobs involving human interaction.

Israeli kibbutzim have for years tried to remove the sex stereotyping of boys and girls. Children's clothes, shoes, hairstyles and lifestyles were fashioned on one sexless, neutral model. Boys were encouraged to play with dolls, sew, knit, cook and clean, and girls were motivated to play football, climb trees and play darts.

The idea of the kibbutz was to have a sexually neutral society in which there were no rigid formulae for each sex and each member had equal opportunity and equal responsibility within the group. Sexist language and phrases like 'big boys don't cry' and 'little girls don't play in the dirt' were removed from the language and kibbutzniks claimed that they could demonstrate a complete interchangeability of roles between the sexes. So, what happened?

After 90 years of kibbutzim, studies have shown that boys in the kibbutz constantly display aggressive and disobedient behaviour, form power groups, fight amongst themselves, form unwritten hierarchies and do 'deals', while girls co-operate with each other, avoid conflicts, act affectionately, make friends and share with one another. Given a free hand to choose their own school courses and subjects, each opted for sex-specific courses, with boys studying physics, engineering and sports, and girls becoming teachers, counsellors, nurses and personnel managers. Their biology directed them to pursuits and occupations that fitted the wiring of their brains.

Studies of neutrally-reared children in these societies show the removal of the mother/child bond does not reduce the sex differences or preferences in children. Rather, it creates a generation of children who feel neglected and confused and are likely to grow into screwed-up adults.

Finally ...

Relationships between men and women work despite overwhelming sex differences. Much of the credit here goes to women because they have the necessary skills to manage relationships and family. They're equipped with the ability to sense the motives and meanings behind speech and behaviour, and can therefore predict outcomes or take action early to avert problems. This factor alone would make the world a much safer place if every nation's leader was a woman. Men are equipped to hunt and chase lunch, find their way home, fire-gaze and procreate – that's it. They need to learn new ways for modern survival just like women do.

Relationships become rocky when men and women fail to acknowledge they are biologically different and when each expects the other to live up to their expectations. Much of the stress we experience in relationships comes from the false belief that men and women are now the same and have the same priorities, drives and desires.

For the first time in human history we are raising and educating boys and girls in identical ways, teaching them that they are the same and that each is as capable as the other. Then, as adults, they get married and wake up one morning to find they are different to each other in every way, shape and form. It's little wonder that young people's relationships and marriages are in such disastrous shape. Any concept that insists on sexual uniformity is fraught with danger because it demands the same behaviour from both men and women, who have quite different brain circuitry. Sometimes it's hard to understand why Nature would plan such apparent incompatibility between the sexes, but it only looks that way because our biology is so at odds with our current environment.

The good news is that when you understand the origins of these differences, you not only find it easier to live with them, you can manage, appreciate, and end up cherishing them too.

Men want power, achievement and sex. Women want relationships, stability and love. To feel upset about this is as useful as abusing the sky for raining. Accepting that it rains allows you to cope with the weather by carrying an umbrella or raincoat, so it is no longer a problem. In the same way, anticipating the difficulties or conflicts that might arise in relationships as a result of our differences enables you to anticipate and defuse them as they occur.

Every day, brain scans are giving us new and exciting insights into how our brains operate and explain many of the things we take for granted. When a girl with anorexia looks in a mirror she sees herself as fat or obese. What she sees is somehow a distortion of her reality. Dr Bryan Lask of London's Great Ormond Street Hospital scanned the brains of anorexic teenagers in 1998 and found that nearly all of them had reduced blood flow to that part of the brain that controls vision. This is just one of dozens of studies that are now uncovering what happens in the brain when things go haywire.

Consistent and solid evidence is coming from scientists everywhere showing that biochemicals in the womb direct the structure of our brains, in turn dictating our preferences. But most of us don't need millions of dollars worth of brain-scanning equipment to know that men don't listen and women can't read maps; the equipment just explains what is often self-evident.

In writing this book, we have presented information that you probably already knew on a subconscious level, but have never stopped consciously to understand.

It's amazing that here, at the beginning of the 21st century, we still don't teach an understanding of male and female relationships in our schools. We prefer to study rats running around mazes or to look at how a monkey will do backflips when conditioned by the reward of bananas. Science is a slow, lumbering discipline and takes years to feed its results into the education system.

So it's therefore up to you, the reader, to educate yourself. For only then can you hope to have relationships as happy and as fulfilling as both men and women deserve.

REFERENCES

Allen, L.S., Richey, M.F., Chai, Y.M. & Gorski, R.A., 'Sex differences in the corpus callosum of the living human being', *Journal of Neuroscience* 11, 933–942 (1991)

Allen, S. & Gorski, R.A., 'Sexual orientation and the size of the anterior commissure in the human brain', *Proceedings of the National Academy of Sciences USA* 89, 7199–7202 (1992)

Amen, Daniel G., *Change Your Brain, Change Your Life: The Breakthrough Program for Conquering Anxiety, Depression, Obsessiveness, Anger, and Impulsiveness*, Times Books (2000)

Andrews, Simon, *Anatomy of Desire: The Science and Psychology of Sex, Love and Marriage*, Little, Brown (2000)

Antes, J.R., McBridge, R.B., & Collins, J.D., 'The effect of a new city route on the cognitive maps of its residents', *Environment and Behaviour* 20, 75–91 (1988)

Archer, John & Lloyd Barbara, *Sex and Gender*, New York: Cambridge University Press (1995)

Bailey, J.M. & Bell, A.P., 'Familiarity of female and male homosexuality', *Behaviour Genetics* 23, 313–322 (1993)

Bailey, J.M. & Pillard R.C., 'A genetic study of male sexual orientation' *Archives of General Psychiatry* 48, 1089–1096 (1991)

Bailey, J.M., Pillard, R.C., Neale, M.C. & Agyei, Y., 'Heritable factors influence sexual orientation in women', *Archives of General Psychiatry* 50, 217–223 (1993)

Baker, Robin, *Sperm Wars: Infidelity, Sexual Conflict and Other Bedroom Battles*, Fourth Estate, Allen & Unwin (1997)

Barash, D., *Sociobiology*, London: Fontana (1981)

Barinaga, M., 'Is homosexuality biological?' *Science* 253, 956–957 (1991)

Baum, M.J., Bressler, S.C., Daum, M.C., Veiga, C.A. & McNamee, C.S., 'Ferret mothers provide more anogental licking to male offspring: possible contribution to psychosexual differentiation', *Physiology and Behaviour* 60, 353–359 (1996)

Beatty, W.W., and Truster, A.I., 'Gender differences in geographical knowledge', *Sex Roles* 16, 565–590 (1987)

Beatty, W.W., 'The Fargo map test: A standardised method for assessing remote memory for visuospatial information', *Journal of Clinical Psychology* 44, 61–67 (1988)

Becker, Jill B., *Behavioural Endocrinology*, Cambridge: MIT Press (1992)

Benbow, C.P. & Stanley, J.C., 'Sex differences in mathematical reasoning ability: more facts', *Science* 222, 1029–1031 (1983)

Berenbaum, S. A.K., & Leveroni, C., 'Early hormones and sex differences in cognitive abilities', *Learning and Individual Differences* 7, 303–321 (1995)

Berrebi, A.S. et al., 'Corpus callosum: Region-specific effects of sex, early experience and age', *Brain Research* 438, 216–224 (1988)

Berry, J. W., 'Temne and Eskimo perceptual skills', *International Journal of Psychology* 1, 207–229 (1966)

Berry, J.W., 'Ecological and social factors in spatial perceptual development', *Canadian Journal of Behavioural Science* 3, 324–336 (1971)

Biddulph, Steve, *Raising Boys*, Berkeley: Celestial Arts (1998)

Biddulph, Steve & Shaaron, *More Secrets Of Happy Children*, New York: HarperCollins (1994)

Blum, Deborah, *Sex on the Brain*, New York: Viking, Penguin (1997)

Booth, A., et al., 'The influence of testosterone on deviance in adulthood: Assessing and explaining the relationship', *Criminology*, Vol. 31 (1), 93–117 (1 Nov 1993)

Botting, Kate & Douglas, *Sex Appeal*, London: Boxtree Ltd. (1995)

Bower, B., 'Genetic clue to male homosexuality emerges' *Science News*, 37 (17 July 1993)

Boyd, R., & Silk J.R., *How Humans Evolved*, New York: Norton (1996)

Brasch, R., *How Did It Begin?*, New York: David McKay (1965)

Brasch, R., *How Did Sex Begin?*, New York: David McKay (1976)

Brown, M.A. & M.J. Broadway, 'The cognitive maps of adolescents: Confusion about inter-town distances', *Professional Geographer* 33, 315–325 (1981)

Burr, C.I., *A Separate Creation*, London, New York: Bantam Press, 167–177 (1996)

Buss, David M., *The Evolution of Desire*, New York: Basic Books, (1994)

Buss, D.M., *The Evolution of Desire: Strategies of Human Mating*, London: HarperCollins, 84–85 (1994)

Cabot, Dr. Sandra, *Don't Let Your Hormones Rule Your Life*, Sydney, Australia: Women's Health Advisory Service (1991)

Carper, Jean., *Your Miracle Brain*, New York: HarperCollins (2000)

Casey, M.B., Brabeck, M.M. & Nuttall, R.L., 'As the twig is bent: The biology and socialisation of gender roles in women', *Brain and Cognition* 27, 237–246 (1995)

Chang, K.T., & Antes, J.R., 'Sex and cultural differences in map reading', *The American Cartographer* 14, 29–42 (1987)

Coates, Jennifer, *Women, Men and Language*, 2d ed., New York: Longman (1993)

Collis, Jack, *Yes You Can*, Australia: HarperCollins (1993)

Crick, Francis, *The Astonishing Hypothesis*, New York: Macmillan (1994)

Crick, F., & Koch, C., 'Are we aware of neural activity in primary visual cortex?', *Nature* 375, 121–123 (1995)

Dabbs, J. M., 'Age and Seasonal Variation in Serum Testosterone Concentration Among Men', *Chronobiology International*, Vol. 7 (3), 245–9 (1990)

Dabbs, J. M., et al., 'Testosterone, crime and misbehaviour among 692 male prison inmates', *Pergamon*, Vol 18 (5), 627–633 (1995)

Dabbs, J. M., 'Testosterone, aggression and delinquency', *Second International Androgen Workshop* 18–20 (Feb 1995)

Damasio, Antonio R., *Descartes' Error: Emotion, Reason, and the Human Brain*, Avon Books (1995)

Darwin, Charles, *The Voyage of the Beagle*, New York: Doubleday (1962)

Darwin, C., *The Descent of Man,* London: Murray, 569 (1871)

Dawkins, Richard, *The Blind Watchmaker,* New York: Norton (1987)

Dawkins, Richard, *The Selfish Gene,* 2d ed., New York: Oxford University Press (1990)

Dawkins, R., 'Universal Darwinism', in Bendall, D. S. (ed.), *Evolution from Molecules to Man,* New York: Cambridge University Press (1983)

Dawkins, R., *River out of Eden: A Darwinian View of Life,* New York: Basic Books (1995)

Deacon, Terrence, *The Symbolic Species: The Co-Evolution of Language and the Brain,* New York: Norton (1997)

DeAngelis, Barbara, *Secrets About Men Every Woman Should Know,* New York: Dell (1991)

DeJong, F. H., and Van De Poll, N. E., *Relationship Between Sexual Behaviour in Male and Female Rats: Effects of Gonadal Hormones,* New York: Elsevier (1984)

De Lacoste, M.C., Holloway, R.L. & Woodward, D. J., 'Sex differences in the fetal corpus callosum', *Human Neurobiology 5,* 93–96 (1986)

De Lacoste-Utamsing, C. & Hollaway, R.L., 'Sexual dimorphism in the human corpus callosum', *Science* 216, 1431–1432 (1982)

Denenberg, V.H., Fitch, R.H., Schrott, L. M., Cowell, P.E. & Waters, N.S., 'Corpus callosum: interactive effects of infantile handling and testosterone in the rat', *Behavioural Neuroscience* 105, 562–566 (1991)

DeVries, G.J., DeBruin, J.P.C., Uylings, H.B.M., and Corner, M.A., (eds.), *Differences in the Brain, Relationship Between Structure and Function,* New York: Elsevier (1984)

Diamond, Jared., *The Third Chimpanzee,* New York: HarperCollins (1992)

Dixon, N., *Our Own Worst Enemy,* London: Futura (1988)

Dorner, G., 'Prenatal Stress and Possible Aetiogenetic Factors of Homosexuality in Human Males', *Edokrinologie* 75, 365–368 (1980)

Dubovsky, Steven L., *Mind–Body Deceptions,* New York: Norton (1997)

References

Eckert, E.D., Bouchard, T.J., Bohlen, J. & Heston, L.L.,
'Homosexuality in monozygotic twins reared apart', *British
Journal of Psychiatry* 14, 421–425 (1986)

Edelson, Edward, *Francis Crick and James Watson and the Building
Blocks of Life*, New York: Oxford University Press (1998)

Edwards, Betty, *The New Drawing on the Right Side of the Brain*,
J P Tarcher (1999)

Ehrhardt, A.A., and Meyer-Bahlburg, H. F. L., 'Effects of prenatal sex
hormones on gender-related behaviour', *Science* 211, 1312–1314
(1981)

Ellis, Havelock, *Man and Woman*, North Stratford, NH: Ayer (1974)

Ellis, Lee, *Research Methods on the Social Sciences*, Minot State
University (1994)

Farah, Martha J., 'Is visual imagery really visual? Overlooked
evidence from neurophychology', *Psychological Review* 95,
307–317 (1988)

Farrell, Dr Elizabeth, & Westmore, Ann, *The HRT Handbook*,
Australia: Anne O'Donovan (1993)

Fast, Julius and Bernstein, Meredith, *Sexual Chemistry: What It Is,
How to Use It*, New York: M. Evans (1983)

Fisher, Helen, *The First Sex*, London: Random House (1999)

Fisher, Helen E., *Anatomy of Love*, New York: Norton (1992)

Fisher, H. W., *Anatomy of Love: The Natural History of Monogamy,
Adultery, and Divorce*, New York: Norton (1992)

Freud, Sigmund, *Three Contributions to the Theory of Sex*, New
York: Random House (1905)

Gardner, Howard, *Extraordinary Minds*, New York: Basic Books
(1998).

Garner, Alan, *Conversationally Speaking*, 2d ed., Los Angeles: Lowell
House (1997)

Gazzaniga, Michael S., (ed.) *The New Cognitive Neurosciences*, MIT
Press (1999)

Ghiglieri, Michael P., *The Dark Side of Man*, Perseus Books (1999)

Gilmartin, P.P., 'Maps, mental imagery, and gender in the recall of
geographical information', *The American Cartographer* 13,
335–344 (1986)

Gilmartin, P.P. & Patton, J.C., 'Comparing the sexes on spatial abilities; map-use skills', *Annals of the Association of American Geographer* 74, 605–619 (1984)

Glass, Lillian, *He Says, She Says*, New York: Putnam (1992)

Gochros, Harvey, & Fischer, Joel, *Treat Yourself to a Better Sex Life*, Englewood Cliffs, NJ: Prentice Hall (1986)

Goffman, Erving, *Gender Advertisements*, New York: Harper (1976)

Goleman, Daniel, *Emotional Intelligence: Why It Can Matter More Than IQ*, New York: Bantam (1997)

Gorski, R.A., 'Sex differences in the rodent brain: their nature and origin', in Reinsch, J.M., et al. (eds.), *Masculinity and Femininity*, Oxford University Press, 37–67 (1987)

Gray, John, *Mars and Venus in the Bedroom*, New York: HarperCollins (1995)

Gray, John, *Men Are From Mars, Women Are From Venus*, New York: HarperCollins (1993)

Gray, John, *Men, Women & Relationships*, 2d ed., Hillsboro, OR: Beyond Words (1993)

Gray, John, *What Your Mother Couldn't Tell You and Your Father Didn't Know*, New York: HarperCollins (1994)

Greenfield, Susan, *The Human Brain: A Guided Tour*, New York: Basic Books (1997)

Greenfield, Susan, *The Human Mind Explained: An Owner's Guide to the Mysteries of the Mind*, New York: Henry Holt (1996)

Greenfield, Susan, *Journey to the Centers of the Mind*, New York: Basic Books (1998)

Grice, Julia, *What Makes a Woman Sexy*, New York: Dodd, Mead

Gur, R. & Gur, R., 'Sex and handedness differences in cerebral blood flow, during rest and cognitive activity', *Science* 217, 659–661 (1982)

Haig, D., 'Genetic imprinting and the theory of parent–offspring conflict', *Developmental Biology* 3, 153–160 (1992)

Hampson, E. & Kimura, F., 'Reciprocal effects of hormonal fluctuations on human motor and perceptospatial skills', *Research Bulletin* 656, Department of Psychology, University of Western Ontario, London, Ontario, Canada (June 1987)

Hampson, E. & Kimura, D., 'Sex differences and hormonal influences on cognitive function in humans', in Becker, J.B., Breedlove, S.M. & Crews, D. (ed.), *Behavioural Endocrinology*, Cambridge, Massachusetts: MIT Press, 357–400 (1992)

Handy, Charles, *The Empty Raincoat: Making Sense of the Future*, London: Hutchinson (1994)

Harlow, H. F. & Zimmerman, R. R., 'The development of affectional responses in infant monkeys', *Journal of the American Philosophical Society* 102, 501–509 (1958)

Harpending, H., 'Gene frequencies, DNA sequences, and human origins', *Perspectives in Biology and Medicine* 37, 384–395 (1994)

Hatfield, E. & Rapson, R. L., *Love, Sex and Intimacy: Their Psychology, Biology, and History*, New York: HarperCollins (1993)

Hendrix, Harville, Ph.D., *Getting the Love You Want: A Guide for Couples*, New York: HarperCollins (1990)

Henley, Nancy M., *Body Politics: Power, Sex and Nonverbal Communication*, Englewood Cliffs, NJ: Prentice Hall (1977)

Henry, W.A. III, 'Born gay?', *Time*, 44–47 (26 July 1993) See also; Maddox, J., 'Is homosexuality hard-wired?', *Nature* 353, 13 (1991)

Hite, Shere, *Women and Love*, New York: Knopf (1987)

Hobson, J.Allan, *The Chemistry of Conscious States: How the Brain Changes Its Mind*, Boston: Little, Brown (1994)

Hobson, J.Allan, *Consciousness*, New York: W.H. Freeman (1998)

Hoyenga, Katharine, Blick, and Kermit T. Hoyenga, *The Question of Sex Differences*, Boston: Little, Brown (1979)

Hoyenga, K.B., Hoyenga, K. T., *Gender-Related Differences*, Allyn & Bacon, 343–345 (1993)

Hoyenga, op cit., 321–2; Mann, V., et al., 'Sex differences in cognitive abilities: A cross-cultural perspective', *Neuropsychologia*, Vol.28, 1063–1077 (1990)

Hu, S., et al., ' Linkage between sexual orientation and chromosome Xq28 in males but not females', *Nature Genetics* 11, 248–256 (1995)

Humphrey, Nicholas, *A History of the Mind*, New York: Simon & Schuster (1992)

Humphrey, Nicholas, 'Contrast Illusions in Perspective', *Nature* 232, 91–93 (1970)

Hutchinson, John B. (ed.), *Biological Determinants of Sexual Behaviour*, New York: John Wiley (1978)

Huxley, Aldous, *The Doors of Perception*, New York: Harper (1963)

Jensen, Eric, *Brain-Based Learning*, Brain Store Inc. (2000)

Johnson, Gary, *Monkey Business*, Gower Publishing (1995)

Kagan, J., 'Sex differences in the human infant', in McGill, Thomas E. et al. (ed.), *Sex and Behaviour: Status and Prospectus*, New York: Plenum (1978)

Kahn, Elayne J., and Rudnitsky, David A., *Love Codes: How to Decipher Men's Secret Signals About Romance*, New York: NAL-Dutton (1992)

Katz, J. N., *The Invention of Homosexuality*, New York: Dutton (1993)

Kimura, D., 'Are men's and women's brains really different?', *Canadian Psycol.* 28 (2), 133–147 (1987)

Kimura, D., 'Estrogen replacement therapy may protect against intellectual decline in post-menopausal women', *Hormones and Behaviour*, 29, 312–321 (1995)

Kimura, D., 'How Different are the male and female brains?', *Orbit*, 17, no.3, 13–14 (October 1986)

Kimura, D., 'Sex differences in the brain', *Scientific American* 267, 118–125 (1992)

Kimura, D., 'Sex differences in the brain', *Scientific American*, 119 (1992)

Kimura, D., 'Sex, sexual orientation and sex hormones influence human cognitive function', *Current Opinion in Neurobiology* 6, 259–263 (1996)

Kimura, D., 'Male brain, female brain: The hidden difference', *Psychology Today*, 51–58 (November 1985)

Kimura, D. & Hampson E., 'Cognitive pattern in men and women is influenced by fluctuations in sex hormones', *Current Directions in Psychological Science* 3, 57–61 (1994)

Kimura, D. & Harshman, R., 'Sex differences in brain organisation for verbal and non-verbal function', *Progress in Brain Research* 61,

De Vreis, G. J. et al. (eds.), Amsterdam: Elsevier, 423–440 (1984)

Kimura, Doreen, *Neuromotor Mechanisms in Human Communication*, New York: Oxford University Press (1993)

King, Dr. Rosie, *Good Loving, Great Sex*, Australia: Random House (1997)

Kinsey, A.C., Pomeroy, W.B. & Martin, C.E., *Sexual Behaviour in the Human Male*, Philadelpia: Saunders (1948)

Kumler and Butterfield, *Gender Difference In Map Reading*, University of Colorado (1998)

Lakoff, Robin, *Language and Woman's Place*, New York: Harper (1976)

LeVay, S. & Hamer, H., 'Evidence for a biological influence in male homosexuality', *Scientific American* 269, 20–25 (May 1994)

LeVay, S., 'A difference in hypothalamic structure between hetero sexual and homosexual men', *Science* 253, 1034–1037 (1991)

LeVay, S., *The Sexual Brain*, Cambridge, Massachusetts: MIT Press (1993)

Lewis, C., et al., 'The prevalence of specific arithmetic difficulties and specific reading difficulties in 9 to 10 year old boys and girls', *Journal of Child Psychological Psychiatry*, Vol.35 (2), 283–292 (1994)

Lewis, David, *The Secret Language of Success*, New York: Carroll & Graf (1990)

Lewis, Michael, 'Culture and gender roles: There is no unisex in the nursery', *Psychology Today* 5, 54–57 (1972)

Lewis, Michael, and Cherry, Linda, 'Social behaviour and language acquisition', in Lewis, Michael and Leonard A. (ed.), Rosenblum *Interaction, Conversation, and the Development of Language*, New York: John Wiley (1977)

Lloyd, B. and Archer, J., *Sex and Gender*, London: Penguin Books (1982)

Logie, R. H., *Visuospatial Working Memory*, Hillsdale, N. J. Erlbaum (1995)

Lorenz, Konrad, *King Solomon's Ring*, New York: Crowell (1952)

Lorenz, Konrad, *On Aggression*, New York: Harcourt (1974)

Maccoby, Eleanor, and Jacklin, Carol N., *The Psychology of Sex Differences*, Stanford: Stanford University Press (1974)

Mack, C. M., Boehm, G. W., Berrebi, A.S. & Denenberg, V. H., 'Sex differences in the distribution of axon types within the genu of the rat corpus callosum', *Brain Research* 697, 152–156 (1995)

Marcel, A.J., 'Conscious and preconscious perception: Experiments on visual masking and word recognition', *Cognitive Psychology* 15, 197–237 (1983)

Marr, D. & Nishihara, H. K., 'Representation and recognition of the spatial organization of three-dimensional shapes', *Proceedings of the Royal Society of London*, B, 200, 269–294 (1978)

Martin P., *The Sickening Mind*, HarperCollins (1998)

Maynard-Smith, John, *Did Darwin Get It Right?*, New York: Penguin (1993)

Maynard Smith, J., *The Theory of Evolution*, New York: Cambridge University (1975/1993)

McCormick, C.M., Witelson, S.F. & Kingstone, E., 'Left-handedness in homosexual men and women: Neuroendocrine implications', *Psychoneuroendocrinology* 15, 69–76 (1990)

McGee, M.G., *Human spatial abilities; Sources of sex differences*, New York: Praeger Press (1979)

McGuiness, D., 'How schools discriminate against boys', *Human Nature*, 82–88 (February 1979)

McKinlay, Deborah, *Love Lies*, London: HarperCollins (1994)

Millard, Anne, *Early Man*, London: Pan (1981)

Miller, Geoffrey F., *The Mating Mind: How Sexual Choice Shaped the Evolution of Human Nature*, London: Doubleday (2000)

Miller, S.K., 'Gene hunters sound warning over gay link', *New Scientist*, 4–5 (24 July 1993)

Moir, Anne, & Jessel, David, *BrainSex*, New York: Dell (1992)

Money, J., 'Ablatio penis: normal male infant sex-reassignment as a girl', *Archives of Sexual Behaviour* 4, 65–71 (1975)

Money, J. & Erhdardt, A.A., *Man and Woman, Boy and Girl: The Differentiation and Dimorphism of Gender Identity from Conception to Maturity*, Baltimore, Maryland: Johns Hopkins University Press (1972)

Money, J. & Erhdart, A.A., 'Progestin-induced hermaphroditism: I.Q. and psychosexual identity in the study of ten girls', *Journal of Sex*

Research 3, 83–100 (1967)

Montagu, Ashley, *Touching: The Human Significance of Skin*, New York: Harper (1971)

Moore, C.L., 'Maternal behaviour of rats is affected by hormonal condition of pups', *Journal of Comparative and Physiological Psychology* 1, 123–129 (1982)

Morris, Desmond, *Animalwatching*, New York: Crown (1990)

Morris, Desmond, *Babywatching*, New York: Crown (1992)

Morris, Desmond, *Bodywatching*, New York: Crown (1985)

Morris, Desmond, *Intimate Behaviour*, New York: Random House (1971)

Morris, Desmond, *The Naked Ape*, New York: Dell (1980)

Morris, Desmond, *Manwatching*, New York: Abrams (1977)

Moyer, K.E., 'Sex differences in aggression', In Friedman et al. (ed.), *Sex Differences in Behaviour*, New York: John Wiley (1974)

O'Connor, Dagmar, *How to Make Love to the Same Person for the Rest of Your Life and Still Love It*, New York: Bantam (1986)

Ornstein, Robert E., *The Right Mind: Making Sense of the Hemispheres*, New York: Harcourt (1997)

Pattatucci, A.M.L. & Hamer, D.H., 'Development and familiarity of sexual orientation in females', *Behaviour Genetics* 25, 407–420 (1995)

Pease, Allan, *Body Language*, Sydney Australia: Camel Publishing (1979)

Pease, Allan, *Everything Men Know About Women*, Sydney, Australia: Camel Publishing (1986)

Pease, Allan, *Rude And Politically Incorrect Jokes*, London: Pease Training International (1998)

Pease, Allan, *Talk Language*, Sydney, Australia: Camel Publishing (1989)

Pease, Allan & Barbara, *Memory Language*, Sydney, Australia: Pease Learning Systems (1993)

Pease, Raymond, & Dr. Ruth, *Tap Dance Your Way to Social Ridicule*, London: Pease Training International (1998)

Peck, M. Scott, *The Road Less Traveled*, New York: Simon & Schuster (1985)

Pertot, Dr. Sandra, *A Commonsense Guide to Sex*, Sydney, Australia: HarperCollins (1984)

Peters, Brooks, *Terrific Sex in Fearful Times*, New York: St. Martin's Press (1988)

Petras, Kathryn, and Petras, Ross, *The 776 Stupidest Things Ever Said*, New York: Doubleday (1993)

Pillard, R.C. & Bailey, J. M., *Archives of Sexual Behaviour 24*, 1–20 (1195); 'Human sexual orientation has a heritable component', *Human Biology 70*, 347–365 (1998)

Pillard, R.C. & Bailey, J.M., 'A biologic perspective on sexual orientation', *The Psychiatric Clinics of North America 18*, 71–84 (1995)

Pool, R., 'Evidence for homosexuality gene', *Science 261*, 291–292 (1993)

Quillam, Susan, *Sexual Body Talk*, New York: Carroll & Graf (1992)

Rabin, Claire, *Equal Partners, Good Friends: Empowering Couples Through Therapy*, London: Routledge (1996)

Reinisch, June M. and Rosenblum, Leonard (eds.), *Masculinity–Femininity*, New York: Oxford University Press (1987)

Reinisch, J.M. et al. (eds.), *Masculinity and Femininity, The Kinsey Institute Series*, Oxford University Press (1987)

Reisner, Paul, *Couplehood*, New York: Bantam (1994)

Rice, G., Anderson, C., Risch, N. & Evers, G., 'Male homosexuality; Absence of linkage to microsatellite markers at Xq128', *Science 284*, 665–667 (1999)

Ridley, Matt, *The Red Queen: Sex and the Evolution of Human Nature*, New York: Macmillan (1993)

Robbins, Jim, *A Symphony in the Brain : The Evolution of the New Brain Wave Biofeedback*, Atlantic Monthly Pr. (2000)

Roger, L.J., *The Development of Brain and Behaviour in the Chicken'*, Wallingford: CAB International (1995)

Rogers, L.J., 'Behavioural, structural and neurochemical asymmetries in the avian brain; A model system for studying visual development and processing', *Neuroscience and Biobehavioral Reviews 20*, 487–503 (1996)

Rosenblum, L. A., 'Sex Differences in Mother–Infant Attachment in Monkeys', In Friedman, R. et al. (ed.) *Sex Differences in Behaviour*,

New York: John Wiley (1974)

Self, C.M., Gopal, S., Golledge, R.G., and Fenstermaker, S., 'Gender-related differences in spatial abilities', *Progress in Human Geography* 16, 315–342 (1992)

Shapiro, R., *Origins*, London: Pelican (1988)

Shaywitz, Sally and Bennett, *'How is the brain formed?'* *Nature* 373, 607–609 (1995)

Stickels, Terry, *Are You As Smart As You Think? : 150 Original Mathematical, Logical, and Spatial-Visual Puzzles for All Levels of Puzzle Solvers,* Griffin (2000)

Stumpf, H., and Klieme, E., 'Sex-related differences in spatial ability: More evidence for convergence', *Perceptual and Motor Skills* 69 Part 1, 915–921 (1989)

Suter, William and Beatrice, *Guilt Without Sex*, London: Pease Training International (1998)

Swaab, D.F., 'Development of the Human Hypothalamus', *Neurochem Research* (US), Vol.20 (5), 509–519 (May 1995)

Swaab, D.F. & Hofman, M.A., 'An enlarged suprachiasmatic nucleus in homosexual men', *Brain Research* 587, 141–148 (1990)

Swaab, D.F. & Hofman, M.A., 'Sexual differentiation of the human hypothalamus in relation to gender and sexual orientation', *Trends in Neurosciences* 18, 264 270 (1996)

Swaab, D. F. & Hofman, M.A., 'Sexual differentiation of the human brain', *Progress in Brain Research* 61, De Vries, G. J. et al. (eds), Amsterdam: Elsevier (1984)

Tannen, Deborah, *Talking from 9 to 5*, New York: Morrow (1994)

Tannen, Deborah, *That's Not What I Meant,* New York: Ballantine (1986)

Tannen, Deborah, *You Just Don't Understand: Women and Men in Conversation*, New York: Morrow (1990)

Tarr, M. J., 'Rotating objects to recognize them', *Psychonomic Bulletin and Review* 2, 55–82 (1995)

Tarr, M. J., & Pinker, S., 'Mental rotation and orientation-dependence in shape recognition', *Cognitive Psychology* 21, 233–282 (1989)

Thorne, Barrie, Kramarae, Cheris & Henley, Nancy (eds.), *Language, Gender and Society*, Boston: Heinle & Heinle (1983)

Tyler, C. W., 'Cyclopean vision', In Regan, D. (ed.), 'Vision and visual dysfunction', *Binocular Vision*, Vol. 9. New York: Macmillan (1989)

Wegesin, D. J., 'Relation between language lateralisation and spatial ability in gay and straight women and men', *Laterality* 3, 227–239 (1998)

Westheimer, Ruth, *Dr. Ruth's Guide to Good Sex*, New York: Warner (1986)

Whiteside, Robert, *Face Language*, New York: Pocket Books (1974)

Whiteside, Robert, *Face Language II*, Hollywood, FL: Frederick Fell (1988)

Wilson, Edward O., *Sociobiology: The New Synthesis*, Cambridge: Harvard University Press (1975)

Wilson, Glenn D., and Nias, David, *The Mystery of Love*, London: Open Books (1976)

Winston Macauley, Marnie, *Manspeak*, Newport House (1996)

Witleson, S. F., 'The brain connection: The corpus collosum is larger in left handers', *Science* 229, 665–68 (1985)

Witleson, S. F., 'Sex differences in the neurology of cognition: psychological, social, educational and clinical implications', In Sullerot, E. (ed.), *Le Fait Feminin*, Paris: Fayard, 287–303 (1978)

Witleson, S.F., 'Left hemisphere specialisation for language in the newborn brain', 96, 641–46 (1973)

Witleson, S.F., 'Hemispheric specialisation for linguistic and nonlinguistic tactual perception using a dichotomous stimulation technique', *Cortex* 10, 3–7 (1974)

Witleson, S.F., 'Sex and the single hemisphere: specialisation of the right hemisphere for spatial processing', *Science* 193, 425–427 (1976)

Wolf, Naomi, *The Beauty Myth*, New York: Anchor (1992)

Wright, Robert, *The Moral Animal*, New York: Pantheon (1994)

Young, J. Z., *An Introduction to the Study of Man*, New York: Oxford University Press (1971)

Zappia, J.V. & Rogers, L. J., 'Sex differences and the reversal of brain asymmetry by testosterone in chickens', *Behavioural Brain Research* 23, 261–267 (1987)